GRACE REHAB

The Power of Labeling Yourself the Way God Labels You

BILL GIOVANNETTI

GRACE REHAB

The Power of Labeling Yourself the Way God Labels You

✦✦✦
Endurant Press

Dedication

This book is dedicated to every survivor, every courageous soul, and every hero willing to resist the world's bullies, mean girls, abusers, users, exploiters, and unloving parents.

It is for every person who refuses to be a victim.

For all those struggling to shed the demeaning labels of the past.

For those great ones fighting to name themselves as God names them.

You inspire me.

You inspire us all.

CONTENTS

PART ONE: I Am in Christ...

PART TWO: In Christ, I Am...

PART ONE
I Am In Christ...

CHAPTER 1

Labels

A TRUE STORY: I SAW IT WITH my own eyes; I felt it in the pit of my own stomach. I can still feel it.

The place: the crowded cafeteria in my large, urban high school. At that time, the student body hovered around five thousand. We sat in a cavernous hall painted in institutional beige. The sounds of hungry students echoed off hard tile floors and cold Formica tables. French fry grease and coleslaw cups added their distinctive aromas to the human smells permeating every molecule in this imposing factory of knowledge.

The scene: a table full of guys was taunting a girl. She was just trying to put away her lunch tray in peace. The guys released their verbal torpedoes:

"Hey Susan, how did you get so ugly?"

"You're hideous!"

"Your mother should have drowned you when you were born!"

"Hey, Ugly!"

The taunts shot across the room and hit her like punches. The whole lunchroom paused to watch.

Susan's head dropped. She fought back tears. She pretended not to hear. One of the brightest students in the whole school, Susan's life was an exercise in survival of the fittest. On some days, the torment was relentless.

We were acquaintances, but not really friends. We shared a few classes together. I thought that Susan was interesting. We had spoken many times, but nothing memorable. She was very smart—an excellent student and a very nice person.

It didn't matter. Once the sadists in the cafeteria got started, nothing stopped them.

Susan ducked as a coleslaw cup whizzed by and splatted against the wall. She couldn't take any more. Her face distorted by agony, she turned to her attackers and screamed. "Shut up! Shut up! Shut up!"

Like blood dripped into shark-infested waters, Susan's reaction sparked a feeding-frenzy. The boys moved in for the kill. They called her a dog and started howling—like wolves baying at the moon.

My stomach tied in a knot that would take hours to untie. Who's running this place? Where are the lunchroom monitors? Where are the teachers? Should I say something? My heart ached for Susan. I felt powerless.

I didn't feel safe.

Susan ran from the lunchroom, refusing to give anybody the satisfaction of seeing her cry.

I left too, and went on with my classes. Just another day in the big city, public school jungle.

I felt wounded, just for witnessing it. I don't pretend to imagine the devastation that Susan felt for living it.

You've Been Slimed

You've been slimed. Odds are strong you've absorbed your sense of who you are from your family and the culture around you. Odds are also strong those sources don't have the slightest clue of who you are in the eyes of God. So they slap their own labels on you: You're stupid, fat, ugly, short, tall. I wish you'd never been born. Don't bother me. You're a loser. You'll never amount to anything. I wish you were like your brother. Why can't you do anything right? You're evil. Dirty. I never wanted you. Failure.

These labels sink deep inside a person. They can latch onto your tender spirit. They haunt you.

They also have a nasty way of creating self-fulfilling prophecies. Because we are ruined by the lies we believe, especially the lies about who we are.

Let me ask a big question: Who are you?

It's not an easy question. You might answer with your name, your job, your college major. You might tell me your marital status or list your kids. Maybe you'll mention where you live or your nationality or religion.

Really, who are you?

Experts suggest your sense of self is planted in infancy, sprouts in childhood, and blooms in adolescence.

For some, that is very bad news. Unless you were blessed with a remarkably healthy upbringing with excellent parents and kind-hearted peers, and unless you were sheltered from the bombardment of unrealistic body images from media and entertainment, you've been slimed. Odds are strong other people's definitions have heavily influenced your identity, possibly distorting it beyond recognition.

The results can be devastating.

Low self-esteem spawns a host of problems, ranging from depression and addiction, to isolation and self-destruction. Some people seem to reinvent themselves as often as it takes to fill their desperate need for approval. It's hard to look at roving hordes of students – each one perfectly dressed, tatted, spiked, and slouched for their social niche – without feeling again the mayhem of my own quest for identity.

Others give up the quest: I am the loser my parents said I was.

Father of the Year

The Bible serves up a painful example of a clueless, label-making father. About a millennium before Christ, God sent the prophet Samuel to identify the second king of Israel. God was specific: he directed the prophet to a little town called Bethlehem, and to the household of a man named Jesse. God said, "One of Jesse's sons will be the next king; you'll know him when you see him because I'll tell you."

Samuel rolled into town and told Jesse the plan. Jesse was excited. One of his sons would be king! He gathered his handsome sons and paraded them before Samuel. The picture-perfect son, Eliab – with his military

14

bearing and muscular frame – was first. "Nope," said Samuel. "Not him. Bring in the next son."

Son number two came in – tough and ready to lead. "Next!" said Samuel.

Samuel sat in mounting confusion as sons three, four, five, six, and seven were pointlessly paraded before him. Here's how the Bible describes that awkward moment:

> In the same way all seven of Jesse's sons were presented to Samuel. But Samuel said to Jesse, "The LORD has not chosen any of these." (1 Samuel 16:6-10, NLT)

Zero for seven. Wait a minute! God told Samuel that Israel's next king would come from among Jesse's sons, and Jesse paraded all seven of his sons in front of Samuel, but the Lord didn't choose any of them.

What gives?

Samuel scratched his head, and looked a little sideways at Jesse.

> Then Samuel asked, "Are these all the sons you have?" "There is still the youngest," Jesse replied. "But he's out in the fields watching the sheep." "Send for him at once," Samuel said. "We will not sit down to eat until he arrives." (1 Samuel 16:11, NLT)

Father of the Year, right? The prophet said, "Show me all your sons" and Jesse skipped one.

Thanks, Dad.

And even when Samuel stood there, scratching his head, and saying no seven times – even in the awkward silence when everybody was confused – Jesse still didn't pipe up about son number eight.

Crickets.

There are as many negative labels as there are schoolyard bullies, distracted fathers, stoned-out mothers, and snooty captains of the cheerleader squad to invent them: ugly, worthless, evil, skinny, fat, outsider, geek, nerd, loser, four-eyes, cripple, useless, bad, nerd, slut.

Let's not even start with ethnic and racial slurs.

David's label is hard to pinpoint. It's not that Jesse called David any bad names, or cussed him out, or shouted how he was a worthless piece of humanity. No. Jesse said nothing. He simply ignored him.

David's own father labeled him with one of the most painful labels of all: NOBODY. You're dead to me. I don't think about you. I don't spend time with you. I don't listen to you. To me, you are nobody.

Thank God, there was Somebody who had a better name for the young shepherd.

> So Jesse sent for him. He was ruddy and handsome, with pleasant eyes. And the LORD said, "This is the one; anoint him." So as David stood there among his brothers, Samuel took the olive oil he had brought and poured it on David's head. And the Spirit of the LORD came mightily upon him from that day on... (1 Samuel 16:12, 13, NLT)

His dad called David NOBODY, but God called him KING. And God did this in front of the very people who scarcely remembered his name.

Grace Heals Your Identity First

People act out of who they are. Actually, people act out of who they *think* they are. This is the crucial life truth most Christians don't realize. Your pastor can preach a thousand sermons on what you should do, but if who you think you are is messed up, those sermons just bounce off your chest. Your identity determines your actions, and no matter how strong your intentions, you're going to slip right back into your old habits as soon as the coffee wears off.

If people act out of who they are, and if who you are has been slimed, then we're all in trouble. That's because the labels you embrace create self-fulfilling prophecies. If you embrace the label *stupid*, what kind of person do you think you'll be? If you embrace the label *loser*, what kind of life will you create? If you embrace the label that you're *better than* everyone else, you're going to be hyper-competitive and fragile when you lose. If you embrace the label *entitled*, you will be a high-chair tyrant and a permanent victim.

Your lifestyle will always incarnate whatever self-identifying labels you embrace. You really can't avoid it. "Out of the heart flow the issues of life," says wise old Solomon (Proverbs 4:23). And, "For as he thinks in his heart, so is he..." (Proverbs 23:7).

It's virtually impossible to grow up in this broken-down world without being degraded, discouraged, debased, and disheartened by other people's labels. Like a freakish funhouse full of deformed mirrors, your identity is easily twisted beyond recognition.

Enter the identity-correcting nuclear option: the matchless grace of God.

All those labels of doom and defeat were blasted to bits in the flood of Calvary's love. When Jesus Christ died on the cross, he stripped away once for all every demeaning label ever slapped on you by any demented foe. The mean girls have nothing to say to you. The bullies can no longer define you. The stoned out parents and absentee loved ones don't own your emotions. You don't need to spend one nanosecond proving yourself to anybody. Your worth has been settled once for all. God has folded you into his family of faith forever, and has shouted to the heavens, "You are my beautiful child and, in you, I am well-pleased."

> Therefore, if anyone is in Christ, he is a new creation; old things have passed away; behold, all things have become new. (2 Corinthians 5:17)

You are a new person with a new name and a new identity linked to the identity of Jesus Christ. You are in permanent union with him. He covers you with his robe of righteousness, and clothes you in his glory. If you are saved, you are "in Christ," and being "in Christ" is the ultimate label and therefore the ultimate ground of you being normal instead of being a basket case.

Grace rehabs your identity first. That is the secret of all lasting change in your life. People act out of who they think they are, so God's first great work in your heart is to change who you think you are. Because that is the only way to change your actions and to repair your relationships and to install within you a permanent pipeline of joy.

After salvation, the primary way to help people change is by filling their hearts with their riches and identity in Christ.

Grace Rehab

I've written this book for anyone who's been slimed by other people's labels. What if those labels are all wrong? What if those labels are part of the devil's strategy to block your true self from soaring to your God-intended heights?

Welcome to a much-needed spiritual, mental, and emotional rehab of your true identity before God. God wants to create in you a triumphant spirit. This is what happens when you upgrade your heart's operating system from legalism (your performance) to grace (God's performance). With a triumphant spirit, nobody can own you. Nobody can defeat you. You are nobody's victim.

A triumphant spirit results from a "renewed mind" (Romans 12:2). It is what happens when your personal *psychology* is saturated with the biblical *theology* of the love of God.

God is ready to renew you. He's ready to unravel a lifetime of destructive labels from your past. He's eager to weave a whole new sense of self deep inside you. He longs to be a bigger voice to you than any lunchroom sadists or monstrous so-called parents. God offers healing to you, beginning today.

And though a thousand voices within you scream, "This book will never work," or "You're permanently damaged goods," God holds out his hands and promises, "The nations will see your righteousness. Kings will be blinded by your glory. And the LORD will give you a new name" (Isaiah 62:2, NLT).

You are ready for this.

How to Use This Book

You don't have to read this book in order. You can skip straight to Part Two now (page 69).

In Part One, we'll talk about *why* and *how* you've received new labels from God. In Part Two we'll discover those labels one by one and apply them.

If theology makes your head throb, I recommend you skip straight from here to Part Two. You can always read Part One later. Skipping it won't hurt you, and it will give your rehab a running start.

The chapters of Part Two are not meant to be read quickly. They're meant to be savored. Contemplated. Read them slowly. Meditate on the opening quotations. Look up the Additional Scriptures. Pray the Prayer out loud. Modify it as you go. Make it your own.

I'm hoping you'll take at least a day on each chapter in Part Two. It's okay to start there. Jesus loves you if you skip parts. So do I.

But don't skip Part One forever.

Part One makes Part Two firm. It shows why your new identity is more than positive self-talk and more than typical self-help. If Part Two is like a house, Part One is like the foundation. In Part One, we dig into the beautiful theology of Union with Christ. Whatever labels God puts on Jesus Christ, he now puts on you. Amazing to think of it. That's the heart of Part One.

My prayer is that God's grace would become more than an academic concept for you. I pray that his grace would come to define your whole way of viewing yourself, your God, and your world. May the truth of God's grace, the power of the gospel, and the Spirit of Christ blow your mind with your very own Grace Rehab.

One more thing: Susan is now a successful Ph.D. professor in a medical field with a beautiful family and many friends. Grace conquers all.

CHAPTER 2

Definitions

THERE ARE TWO PRIMARY LABELS that define your life. You can trace every bit of dysfunction and every bit of health in your life back to these two labels:

1. How you label yourself.
2. How you label God.

These two labels create self-fulfilling prophecies. You will live up (or down) to whatever labels you put on yourself. And God will live up (or down) – in your experience – to whatever labels you put on him.

There's a beautiful story in the Bible in which God chased down a leader-in-hiding that he might rehab both sets of labels.

Picture Moses, the former ruler from the palace of Egypt, now tending flocks in the desert. God grabbed his attention with a burning bush, and commissioned him to return to Egypt. Moses was destined to set his people free.

How incredible! Moses had been in hiding for forty years. Forty years of running from a guilty past. Forty years of keeping a low profile. Forty years of labeling himself a useless cog in a pointless cosmic machine.

Countless people would identify with him today. Perhaps even you.

From a burning bush, God called to Moses, just like he calls to you. "I have a great plan for you. I have something for you to live for, and something worth even dying for. I believe in you," God said.

How would you respond to such a call from God?

Here's how Moses responded:

"But who am I to appear before Pharaoh?" Moses asked God. "How can you expect me to lead the Israelites out of Egypt?" (Exodus 3:11, NLT)

But Moses protested again, "Look, they won't believe me! They won't do what I tell them. They'll just say, 'The LORD never appeared to you.'" (Exodus 4:1, NLT)

But Moses pleaded with the LORD, "O Lord, I'm just not a good speaker. I never have been, and I'm not now, even after you have spoken to me. I'm clumsy with words." (Exodus 4:10, NLT)

But Moses again pleaded, "Lord, please! Send someone else." (Exodus 4:13, NLT)

Can you see why labels are so important?

God said, "Moses, I believe in you for great things!"

Moses said, "But. But. But. But." Four times. Moses slapped big fat labels over his forehead: Inadequate. Unworthy. Stuttering. Guilty.

God designed you to soar, but labels make you limp.

It gets worse.

It's a short and inevitable step from mis-labeling yourself to mis-labeling God. Your negative labels of yourself somehow begin to stick to God: He's an ogre. Heartless. Distant. Weak. A non-entity. Exploiter. Bully.

Who are you?

Who is God to you?

Moses didn't even know what to call God. He was born a Jew, raised an Egyptian, and lived in Midian. God was lost to him. He asked the question that we all ask one way or another: Who are you, God?

God answered him.

> But Moses protested, "If I go to the people of Israel and tell them, 'The God of your ancestors has sent me to you,' they won't believe me. They will ask, 'Which god are you talking about? What is his name?' Then what should I tell them?" God replied, "I AM THE ONE WHO ALWAYS IS. Just tell them, 'I AM has sent me to you.'" God also said, "Tell them, 'The LORD, the God of your ancestors–the God of Abraham, the God of Isaac, and the God of Jacob–has sent me to you.' This will be my name forever; it has always been my name, and it will be used throughout all generations." (Exodus 3:13-15, NLT)

Moses asked, "Who are you, Lord? What is your name?"

God told him.

Why? Because God was starting the healing of Moses by putting the correct label on himself. You can't label yourself right until you label God right.

Who Am I?

Moses asked, "Who am I?" You ask the same question every time you get in trouble, run out of money, fight with your spouse, or break up with your boyfriend or girlfriend. Who am I? You ask that every time you flunk a test, and feel lost in math class. Who am I? That's what you ask when you lose your home, your job, your friends, your love, your health, or your familiar places.

An identity crisis.

Who am I? What good am I? Who cares?

Immediately the Evil Label-Maker, called the devil, rushes in with a long list of suggestions. Your peer group adds their suggestions. The media and TV add their suggestions. The legalistic, ultra-religious people in your life add their suggestions. Voices from your past chime in, too.

Pretty soon you're plastered with labels calling you a failed, hideous, worthless pile of steaming dung who will never enjoy the life of your dreams.

You picked up this book, by God's plan, so you could discover this simple truth: *all of those labels are lies.*

We are ruined by the lies we believe, but there's good news. We are healed by the truths we seize. You can shed the lies.

The only one who knows the real you – the deep you, the true you – is God. Your Heavenly Father knows who you are. He calls you by your true name, not by the degrading names others have slapped on you.

He calls you by your true, glorious, beautiful, holy, beloved, honorable, valuable, precious, wise, more-than-adequate, powerful, intelligent, just-right name.

When you call him by his name, God calls you by your name. You may be ruined by the lies you believe, but you can be healed by the truths you seize.

There's a kind of teaching in many churches called "name it and claim it," as if you can make yourself rich by just believing hard enough. Not so. That's a false teaching.

But there is a true "name it and claim it" in the Bible, and here's how it goes: *On the day God saved you, Jesus Christ claimed you as his own and names you as you really are.* And that is the only "name it and claim it" the Bible knows.

This is your time, your moment to shed the labels of a lifetime and let your true self shine. You are who God says you are. You are the richest person you know. You are cherished and precious in his sight. You can be all God designed you to be, all that you dream of being, and so much more. You can bear within you the shimmering power of a triumphant spirit.

It's time to peel back the lies.

It's time to learn your real name.

Who are you?

Let's find out.

CHAPTER 3

Union

THE WHO AM I QUESTION plagued me from my freshman year in high school. My teacher stumped me with it. I didn't know where to begin. The assignment seemed simple enough, but the more I thought about it, the less I knew what to write. My English teacher, on the first day of my high school career, assigned a six-page paper entitled, "Who Am I?"

Beside my name and other particulars, I had no idea what to say.

That afternoon, I stared at a blank paper for a long while. My name clacked off my old-fashioned typewriter. I offered up the amazing fact I was from Chicago. And my favorite food was steak.

Pathetic.

How in blazes could I possibly fill six pages with the story of a life just beginning? And who the heck was I anyway?

That night, I went to church. My very cool, hip, cute piano teacher walked by. We were standing in the basement, at the bottom of a stairway, where bathroom doors flanked a lukewarm drinking fountain. Fluorescent lights buzzed above and the sounds of old people at prayer filtered in from the multi-purpose room. Though Celeste was impossibly old – at least twenty-two at the time – I still had a minor crush on her.

"Hi Celeste."

"Hi Bill. You look miserable."

"Really?" I adjusted my face – not an easy task. "Well, I have this paper due tomorrow. I don't have a clue what to write." I took a sip from the drinking fountain and wiped my face.

"What's it on?"

"It's stupid actually..."

Celeste tipped her head and asked again, "What's your paper about?"

"Who Am I? It's supposed to be about who I am."

Celeste didn't miss a beat. "I am a child of God, a servant of the living King. I am adopted. I am accepted. I am beloved. I am..."

The lights went on, not only for my paper, but also for my whole life.

Though I've doubted my true identity a million times since that day, I have never budged from the mother of all psychological/theological premises: *I am who God says I am now that I belong to Christ.* I had learned it in Sunday School – *academically* – but that encounter with Celeste planted seeds that would take root and grow up into a grace-filled sense of self *emotionally. Spiritually.*

That night, I went home and wrote a paper about my identity in Christ.

My Chicago public high school teacher gave me an A, without comment.

In Christ

The Bible serves up its most common designation of a Christian in a concise two-word packet: "in Christ." By definition, a Christian is a person who is "in Christ" or "in Him."

Here's what that means.

When you received Jesus as your Savior, God did something remarkable and irreversible: he joined you to Christ. A few drops of divine super-glue, and done. This joining did not obliterate your personality or turn you into a Christian zombie; it unshackled your true self – your deepest personality – and made it possible for you to be the best you, with all the color added.

Bible scholars call this the Doctrine of Union with Christ. The great Princeton theologian, John Murray, declared: "Union with Christ is the central truth of the whole doctrine of salvation."[1]

When Celeste solved my Who Am I dilemma, she was applying the doctrine of union with Christ to my sense of self. Union with Christ is to self-acceptance as screaming teenage girls are to the latest teen-idol's concert: inseparable.

How does it work?

Who God Says You Are

When you received Christ as your Savior, God plunged you into Christ. He made you one with Christ. Salvation is a very big deal. It completely blows your pre-Jesus identity out of the water, and recreates a whole new self.

Before meeting Jesus, I was plain, solitary Bill. Just me. Bill plus zero.

Now that I have Jesus as my Savior, I am Bill plus Christ forever. I've been fused to him, so to speak. My old identity is gone – Bill plus zero no longer exists. Only the new one remains, Bill plus Christ. As weird as it might sound, this is a very good thing.

The Bible uses the words "in Christ" or "in him" to indicate this. Here's one of many examples: "There is therefore now no condemnation to those who are in Christ Jesus..." (Romans 8:1). To be in Christ is to be free from condemnation, once for all.

See how that works?

Buckle your seat belt, because the implications are astounding. You are so joined to Jesus Christ that whatever God says about Jesus, he now says about you.

Let that sink in. If God were to describe you today, what would he say? If he were to stand up in the throne room of heaven, command the silence of the worshipping angels and feasting saints, and say, "Today, I'm going to tell you all about [insert your name here,]" what would that celestial speech sound like?

If you are in Christ, he would describe you in the same terms he would use to describe Jesus.

What does God say about Jesus? Is he beautiful? Is he acceptable? Is he valuable? Is he powerful?

Then you are too.

What would God never say about Jesus? I hate you? I don't want you? You're ugly? Leave me alone? You're stupid? No, of course not, never in a million times a million millennia. It's unthinkable.

If he would never say those things about Jesus, then he would never say, or even think, those things about you. You are one with Christ.

When God joined you to Christ, he erased every demeaning label that every schoolyard bully, every mean girl, every stoned parent, and every religious hypocrite ever spray-painted across your heart. You are not ugly. You are not stupid. You are not worthless. You are not anything the world says you are.

You are who God says you are.

And he says you are in permanent union with the best person whose leather sandals ever trudged the dusty streets of planet earth.

I know this sounds like abstract theology with as much practical value as a moon rock on your mantel, but please stay tuned. We are laying down the only biblical rails that support the train of a self-acceptance that means something and outlasts your episodes of embarrassing behaviors.

By this union with Christ, God launched your status, your name, your nature, and your potential into the stratosphere.

Its Nature

Here are some important qualities of your union with Christ.

Your union with Christ is *permanent*. There is no "undo" command. At some weddings, the bride and groom pour colored sand into a vase. The bride pours in one color; the groom pours in another. They do this together, so the grains of sand intermingle in the vase. The idea is that two are becoming one in a way that can't be undone.

Though God is perfectly capable of separating multi-colored grains of sand, he will never separate you from Christ. He promised. No power in heaven above, earth below, or hell beneath "shall be able separate us from the love of God which is in Christ Jesus our Lord" (Romans 8:39).

Your union with Christ is also *instantaneous*. Like super-glue, the bond is immediate. You don't grow into it. It doesn't harden over time. You are as "in Christ" on Day One of your salvation as you will be a thousand eons from now in heaven. In the language of theology, union with Christ is not a *process*, it is a *crisis*. It's a sudden turning point, a before-and-after moment, with the "before" picture obliterated, and the "after" picture spotlighted for the rest of forever.

Your union with Christ is also *invisible* and *non-sensory*. When I was younger, I struggled because I didn't feel anything when I got saved. No tingles. No organ music from heaven. No sparks flying. What if it didn't "take"?

God sent a wise teacher into my life named Bill Bright. His little booklet offered an illustration: a train with an engine, coal car, and caboose. Bill Bright labeled the engine FACTS, the coal car FAITH, and the caboose FEELINGS. He pointed out that a train could run without its caboose, but not without an engine or coal car.[2]

Feelings are optional, he was saying.

It's nice if they're there, but not necessary.

I learned being placed into union with Christ is a work of God in the spiritual realm. You don't feel it, hear it, taste it, smell it, or see it. It has no official feeling. It does, however, come with overwhelming scriptural support, so we take it as fact by faith and move on, no matter how we feel. If you have received Christ, you are joined to Christ, for better or worse, heartburn or health, laughter or tears, no emotion at all or "joy unspeakable and full of glory" (1 Peter 1:8, KJV).

Your union with Christ is also *total*. It comes to you as an entire package, lacking nothing. God adds no parts to it as time goes on because all the parts were there on Day One. No assembly required. God looks at you through Christ-colored lenses, and every part of you is beautiful in his sight. Scripture declares you to be "complete in Him" (Colossians 2:10). This momentous event called salvation slathers you with goodness beyond your wildest dreams.

Seriously?

By now, you might be rolling your eyes, objecting: "Wait one minute, Mr. Holy Man! On the days I can't squeeze into my fat-jeans, and I'm pounding down Thin Mint cookies faster than a gator on a Yorkie, and self-loathing rises with the cholesterol in my veins, you're telling me that a dusty old doctrine of union with Christ is going to make a difference?"

Actually, no.

I'm telling you that God is going to make a difference by rehabbing all the mental scripts that make you so insecure to begin with. And he uses this dusty old doctrine to do it.

The rehab begins with a realistic appraisal of your truest self.

And said self can only be found in union with Christ.

That's what I'm telling you.

"Okay, Smart Guy," you might concede. "You just said union with Christ is invisible and non-sensory and all that, so how can it possibly do an atom of good in this agitated life of mine?"

That's easy.

Let's see how it works.

CHAPTER 4

Seed

YOUR UNION WITH CHRIST grows like a seed planted in your soul, spreading vines into your mind and emotions and from there into your relationships, marriage, parenting, career, and everything else about you. The *reality* of your union with Christ is total and complete. Your *realization* of it happens gradually over time.

You obtain a new *life*; that's first.

You attain a new *lifestyle*; that's second.

Scholars describe union with Christ in three overlapping circles:

1. A Legal Union

In traditional wedding vows, the man says, "With all of my earthly goods, I thee endow." In that moment she becomes joint owner of all his stuff, including his credit card debts. Even if she didn't pile up those debts, they're hers. Ditto for his wealth. This works both ways. The woman owns the man's assets and liabilities just as a man owns the woman's. A husband and wife share a legal relationship from the moment the minister signs the license.

That's why God can smell your morning breath and still raise a cheer.

Because all the goodness of Christ became yours the moment you were saved. This was a legal transaction in the courtroom of heaven. God endowed you with all of Christ's earthly and heavenly goods – including what the Bible calls "righteousness." You can see this in places like:

> I will greatly rejoice in the LORD, My soul shall be joyful in my God; For He has clothed me with the garments of salvation, He has covered me with the robe of righteousness... (Isaiah 61:10)

> [A]nd be found in Him, not having my own righteousness, which is from the law, but that which is through faith in Christ, the righteousness which is from God by faith. (Philippians 3:9, KJV)

This gift-package is not something you earn; it's something you receive. It's not an attainment; it's an obtainment. Not something you sweat and strain for, but something you accepted as a free gift the day you accepted Christ. You obtained a new legal status before God, one identical to that of Jesus Christ.

This is part of your new life.

Some Bible experts use the term "Federal Head." They mean that Jesus is the representative of a vast tribe of people. He stands in for them, representing them before heaven's throne. Like a federation of nations, all true Christians are a federation of redeemed people, under the leadership of Jesus. Whatever he brings to the table, heaven recognizes as belonging to his whole tribe.

This is your status, your exalted position, in Christ.

How do you think heaven responds when Jesus approaches God's throne? I imagine angels soaring, saints rejoicing, demons trembling, worship exploding, and God smiling. Heaven goes wild over the one and only person truly worthy "to receive power and riches and wisdom, / And strength and honor and glory and blessing" (Revelation 5:12).

Jesus Christ is worthy. That is his status. And, because of this legal aspect of your union with Christ, it is your status too. His worthiness counts for you. You are married to him, so to speak.

The same wild ovation that cheers Jesus in the halls of heaven also cheers you. His status is your status. His glory is your glory. His spirit of triumph has been implanted within you.

Says who?

Says God. Signed in blood, sealed by omnipotence, shouted to the heavens, and secured for eternity:

> But of Him you are in Christ Jesus, who became for us wisdom from God – and righteousness and sanctification and redemption – that, as it is written, "He who glories, let him glory in the LORD." (1 Corinthians 1:30, 31)

Like a wise, joyful, caring father, God takes your toddler-like hand in his strong grip and walks you across the highway of life's cruelty. He won't let go. He promised.

This legal union cements your status – your rank and privileges – before God in heaven. It locks in place how

God sees you: when he looks at you, he thinks and feels as if he were looking at Christ.

The whole idea is remarkable. No other religion offers anything like it. Instead of burdening you with the need to climb some ladder of perfection, God lifts you by his royal elevator to the heights of glory on Day One of your salvation.

Compare it to a marriage certificate: the certificate is signed; the union has been made, the deed is done. Now the trick is to make this union real in your daily life.

So God pushes your union with Christ deeper than a marriage certificate in the law books of heaven.

2. A Mystical Union

"Jesus is in my heart," he said. "But he's small."

"What do you mean by your heart?" I said.

The nine-year-old pointed to his chest.

"What?" I said.

"You know... this..." he pointed to his chest again. "The thing that pumps my blood."

Brandon, the ten year old in my church's kids club, visualized Jesus in his heart as a miniature "G.I. Jesus" swimming inside the organ that pumped his blood. Physically. Concretely. An idea meaningless at best, and freakish at worst, though completely understandable in a kid.

Yes, Christ lives in you, but not physically. He dwells in you spiritually in a mystical way that cannot be fully defined. If the legal union offers you a oneness of *status* with Christ, the mystical union offers a oneness of *heart* with him.

We could say the legal union plus the mystical union equals your new life in Christ. The instant he moved in, he redefined you.

This indwelling is not physiological, as if we could dissect your corpse some day to free mini-Jesus. It is a spiritual truth, impossible to quantify, and a great mystery:

> To them God willed to make known what are the riches of the glory of this mystery among the Gentiles: which is Christ in you, the hope of glory. (Colossians 1:27)

"Christ lives in me," said St. Paul (Galatians 2:20).

"Do you not know yourselves, that Jesus Christ is in you?" he asked (2 Corinthians 13:5).

When you got salvation, you also got Jesus. Let's call this Christ's "indwelling." He indwells you that he might live through you. This does not mean you will walk in sandals, grow long hair, or give up bacon. It does not mean you will speak in thee's, thou's, or say keepeth or loveth, or maintain a gloomy look of doom upon your face.

The presence of Christ in you does not suck the personality out of you.

He does not turn you into a clone.

Instead, Christ's presence has everything to do with power, integrity, and wholeness. Jesus came inside you to strengthen you to become the best *you* possible, with all the color added.

Jesus "pressures" you in a good way. He does this from the inside. He does this with love, not guilt. He motivates. He empowers. He delivers his own great strength to operate your life's machinery according to divine instructions.

When a big fat temptation dangles a juicy hook in front of you, he is your strength to turn away.

When Mr. Devil scorches your conscience with accusations, Jesus reminds your memory banks of your forgiveness in him.

When your teenage daughter stomps off in a queenly snit, screeching your awfulness to a house full of mortified guests, Jesus rises up to be your dignity, poise, and grace.

When I was a rookie pastor, a grizzled old veteran said something that wrapped me up like a python. We were holding a baptism service for high-school students in the pristine lake of a Christian camp. As part of the service, each student told the story of how they first encountered Jesus. One girl told her story and added, "And I'm getting baptized today because I want to be closer to Jesus."

An ancient pastor named Lance B. Latham, watching the baptisms, clambered to his feet. He tottered to the microphone and said how excited he was for this girl. Then he gently added, "I want you to know something: You can't get any closer to Jesus Christ than you are right now. He lives inside you. You can't get any closer than that."

Do you see how that could stick with a young pastor?

I hope it sticks with you.

You can't get any closer to Christ than you already are. There's nothing closer than "in."

You can't get any more of Jesus than you already have. He doesn't arrive in parts. The day you received him, you got all of him. His indwelling. His presence. His guidance. His comfort. His power. His life. His everything.

Who am I? The dwelling place of Christ.

Christ Lives In Me

Marinate your mind in these words, because they're a key ingredient in the recipe of biblical self-acceptance:

> I have been crucified with Christ; it is no longer I who live, but Christ lives in me; and the life which I now live in the flesh I live by faith in the Son of God, who loved me and gave Himself for me. (Galatians 2:20)

Let's decode that.

The person I was before I met Jesus – call me Bill – no longer exists as such. I've been "crucified" so to speak. Christ's death counts for me. His death certificate resides forever in my permanent files. That's my legal status. If the devil doesn't like it, he can sue me – but wait, I'm dead! Good luck collecting.

Even so, I live. In what sense? For the rest of forever I will be Bill-plus-Jesus. That is who I am. That's who wrote this book. That's who just downed two cups of Italian Roast coffee. That's who preaches at my church. That's who plays Airsoft with my son, and laughs at my daughter's brilliant one-liners.

Bill-plus-Jesus is the person I bring to the table in my relationships, my family, my home, my career, and my life. There is no such thing as a "Bill" devoid of Christ anymore. I find my identity in Jesus, in my union with him, because there is no alternative me.

By the legal union, God changed my status.

By the mystical union, God changed my identity.

But it goes deeper: Now, by the moral union, God is changing my lifestyle.

3. A Moral Union

On random days, I bring flowers to my wife. She likes this a lot. I like her smile a lot. I love her and she loves me. On most days, we even like each other – though she isn't very happy when I snore.

Honey, it's involuntary.

The legal union is the seed. The mystical union is the root. And the moral union, in which I grow increasingly "conformed" to Christ, is the fruit (Romans 8:29).

This is where God loves me and I love him back in a way I can sense and feel. This is when I worship or serve God in the way an eager kid presents construction-paper art to Mom or Dad. By this moral union I actually begin to resemble who I really am. Christ's wisdom is increasingly my wisdom. His power is my power. His peace is my peace. His courage... Let's just say his everything becomes my everything.

This requires growth.

This makes the moral union dramatically unlike the legal and mystical unions. Those unions happen in an instant. They are instantaneous and they are perfect the moment you cross the threshold of faith. They cannot grow or improve, because you can't improve on perfection.

The moral union, however, is different. It is a process of growth that keeps getting better (hopefully) over time. By this process, you grow deeper and stronger and more assured in your life with God.

You leave better tips at Denny's.

You speak kinder words at home.

You love unlovable people a little more.

You tell the truth.

You feel peace in life's storms.

You experience power in your weakness.

You walk in purity.

You pray.

You enjoy time in God's Word.

What's happening is the moral union. Christ increasingly expresses his life through you. Your oneness of *life* is becoming a oneness of *lifestyle*.

If you've ever seen a flower shove its way through a sidewalk, you understand the power of the new life Jesus brings. He lives in you, by his own power, his own supernatural strength, and his own endless life.

And he doesn't come with an off-switch.

Once you have Jesus, you have a ceaseless impulse inside you to be like him, in your lifestyle. That's why St. Paul could urge you "to walk worthy of the calling with which you were called" (Ephesians 4:1). Make your lifestyle match your life. Live up to your potential. Let your true self, attached to Jesus, shine.

Let the legal union and the mystical union splatter your world in the dazzling colors of Christ-likeness through the moral union.

You are a Christian, so act like Christ.

Which is, of course, impossible by human strength alone. Therefore, God invites you to undergo a total rehab of how you think about yourself. There is no other way to experience your moral union with Christ.

The legal union renewed your status before God, all at once, instantaneously.

The mystical union renewed your identity before God, all at once, instantaneously.

The moral union now renews your self-perception and lifestyle before God and the world, gradually, over time, as you increasingly embrace the first two unions. This happens as you grow up, spiritually speaking. Grow mature. Learn of him. Sink deep roots into "the unsearchable riches of his grace" (Ephesians 3:8). I wrote this book to help nudge that process along.

It's time to renew your mind with the power of God.

It's time for a your grace rehab.

CHAPTER 5

Identity

THIS REHAB REQUIRES a thorough understanding of exactly what does and doesn't belong to you now that you belong to Jesus. Yes, you're one with Christ, but that doesn't make you God. No offense, but I saw you lose it at Walmart, so I'm relieved you're not God.

It works like this: you are joined to Christ in such a way that everything true about Jesus Christ *in his human nature* before the Father is also true of you. This is not to deny his divine nature: he is, was, and always will be fully God. At the same time, he is fully human, and it is this human nature that defines your privileges.

This tasty confection is delivered in four flavors, with countless toppings: you share Christ's status, nature, possessions, and destiny.

Let's sample them one at a time.

Sharing Christ's Status

Picture a religious success story with a spiritual pedigree a mile long. In his religion, he's the rising star. He's the best of the best of the best. He has a Ph.D. from the Harvard of his day. A genius I.Q. A political mastermind. A power-broker with both earthly rulers and with heaven's God.

Now picture him tearing up his diplomas. Imagine him shaking his head in embarrassment for missing the nose on his theological face. And watch him wrapping himself in the religious achievements of Another.

That man would be named Saul of Tarsus, later called Paul. Saint Paul to some, the Apostle Paul to others, and plain Paul to most.

He climbed to the highest echelons of religious leadership in ancient Israel, only to find his ladder leaning against the wrong wall. Paul discovered what every rookie follower of Jesus needs to learn: you've been promoted.

You've even skipped some grades.

Paul put it this way:

> Yet indeed I also count all things loss for the excellence of the knowledge of Christ Jesus my Lord, for whom I have suffered the loss of all things, and count them as rubbish, that I may gain Christ and be found in Him, not having my own righteousness, which is from the law, but that which is through faith in Christ, the righteousness which is from God by faith. (Philippians 3:8, 9)

He counted his exalted human status as "rubbish" in the eyes of God. All he cared about was being "found in him." When you Googled "Paul," he wanted "in Christ" to come up. Whatever achievement he pointed to, whatever success he celebrated, and whatever righteousness he wrapped around his bony shoulders, he wanted it to be Christ's.

For the Christian, your status before God, the angels, and the demons is equal to that of Jesus Christ. If Jesus were a five-star chef, you'd be one too. The other chefs in the kitchen would snap to attention when you barked. If he were a five-star general, you'd be one too. His rank is your rank. Whatever respect heaven pays to Jesus, heaven also pays to you.

Not someday. Not when you've died and gone to heaven. If you are in union with Christ, the angels of heaven salute you, and the demons of hell tiptoe around you right now, today, because Christ's exalted status has already been conferred upon you once-for-all.

No philosopher, no humanitarian, no religion, and no other religious system has ever invented a salvation so beautiful and so dignifying of human nature as the gospel of Jesus Christ.

Sharing Christ's Nature

Sharing Christ's status tells you *who* you are in God's eyes. Sharing his nature tells you *what* you are.

Is Jesus a child of God? In him, you are God's child too.

Is Jesus accepted by God? Then God's acceptance of you is as limitless and eternal as his acceptance of Christ. For anybody who struggles with self-acceptance, it can be hard to realize just how warmly and easily God accepts you, just as you are, right now, today, because you belong to Christ.

Is Jesus beautiful? "So the King will greatly desire your beauty; / Because He is your Lord, worship Him" (Psalm 45:11). In case nobody has ever said it before, you, dear child of God, are beautiful.

Whatever Jesus is, you are, and you always will be.

When my classmates tortured Susan with labels like ugly and dog, they were defining her from their own putrid perspectives. They treated her, not as a person, but as an "it." Trapped in their sins, their naming only spewed forth the toxins of their own depraved souls.

But Susan didn't know that.

To her, the labels spoke a sort of truth. They had to. She was too young to have built the shields to ward off the attack. Unless she was blessed with unusually healthy parents, Susan would have little choice but to absorb the labels into her psyche and do her best to cope.

And to flee the wolf pack.

You have a Father in heaven who sees in you nothing but beauty.

What is Jesus?

He is powerful. He is glorious. He is perfect. He is eternal. He is good. He is accomplished, successful, beloved, capable, and true. He is holy and righteous. He is the standard of all that God demands and accepts in a human being.

In Christ, you are all these things and more.

Even if your earthly dad called you a lazy bum, or your ex- ridiculed your big head. Even if the lunchroom bullies howled at you. They're all lunatics, psychotically broken from reality, and one day God will show them to be the fools they are.

And while he's at it, he will show the entire universe the wonders he has seen in you all along. In Christ, you are perfect in every way.

Sharing Christ's Possessions

How would you like to own mineral rights to the rings around Saturn? What if you knew the proprietary process for nuclear fusion and could harness it for clean energy? When Forbes lists the wealthiest people in the world, every year they miss one. They miss the wealthiest of all. God has bestowed the wealth of the cosmos upon a member of our very own tribe – upon a human, Jesus Christ.

The Bible calls him "heir of all things," a reference to the universe and all the universes of universes (Hebrews 1:2).

You, who might not be able to pay the electric bill and are doing your best to dodge the credit-hounds, have been made a joint-heir with Christ:

> The Spirit Himself bears witness with our spirit that we are children of God, and if children, then heirs – heirs of God and joint heirs with Christ... (Romans 8:16, 17)

Jesus has a lot of wealth. He has gold, silver, and precious stones. The vaults of heaven sparkle with treasures not even an eternal spending binge can dent. The Bible speaks of the "unsearchable riches of Christ," no doubt a reference to his spiritual riches, but certainly true of his material riches, too (Ephesians 3:8). In every category, Jesus tops the charts.

And you are as rich *as him,* because you are rich *in him.*

You are the richest person you know.

It is likely, unfortunately, that you don't *feel* that way. Good thing you're studying this stuff, don't you think? Imagine your life if you could walk into a room full of friends, feeling the security of more wealth than you could burn through in a million lifetimes. The easy confidence of a firstborn's inheritance can be yours.

Does this mean that you will finally get that oceanfront mansion and fully staffed yacht you've been eyeing? Not necessarily. Whatever else it means, you can be sure that God will fill your heart with blessings money can't buy.

God has engraved your name on the title deed to the universe. You are an heir today, and one day you will come into your full inheritance. Until then, God is faithful to prepay as he supplies "all your need according to His riches in glory by Christ Jesus" (Philippians 4:19).

Whatever belongs to Jesus belongs to you.

When that simple truth fills your horizon, you can consider your rehab – and the development of your triumphant spirit – well under way.

Sharing Christ's Destiny

Roller coasters have no steering wheels. That's because they run on tracks from beginning to end. The end is foreordained: in three minutes you'll get there.

When God strapped you into union with Christ, your eternal destiny was taken out of your hands forever. You were placed onto pre-determined tracks: the tracks laid down by God himself for Christ.

There are no steering wheels in sight. Christ's destiny is your destiny. His destination is your destination. You're riding the rails to "Destination: Glory." You're going where he goes, receiving what he receives, and experiencing what he experiences.

In a few decades*, you'll reach the end [*results may vary].

And that end is just the beginning of glories that would so overwhelm your present human capacities that God will have to prep you. He will grant you a radically upgraded physiology, affectionately dubbed the *resurrection body.* In your resurrection body you will enter the blazing presence of a holy God and not get scorched. You will enjoy physical sensations no virtual reality theorist could imagine. You will plunge into overwhelming happiness language can't describe.

A few years ago, I led my family, along with my mother-in-law and her aged sister, on a hike down a woodsy trail. Spider webs crisscrossed the path, freaking out the ladies, and threatening to cut our excursion short. Guess what city-slicker rose to the occasion. I rummaged in the brush for a big stick and took the lead, holding the stick vertically a foot before my face. Between the stick and my face, we collected enough of the spider webs to clear the way for our little troupe.

To an immeasurably greater magnitude, Jesus cleared the way for you to tread the path to heaven, so that you might one day leap headlong into Christ's collection of celestial toys.

Whatever will happen to Jesus Christ, in his human nature, in heaven, will also happen to you. His playground becomes yours. His toy box opens to you. You share his destiny.

Will he have a throne? He'll slide over and invite you to share it with him (Ephesians 2:6).

Will he receive glory? When God lights up Jesus as a spectacle to dazzle the angels, he'll light you up too. You share Christ's immortal glory: "When Christ who is our life appears, then you also will appear with Him in glory" (Colossians 3:4). John promises, "We shall be like him" (1 John 3:2). What a jaw-dropping claim!

Will he enjoy the Father's praise? So will you. There might not be two people on planet earth who would stand and applaud when you entered a room. So what! God does. His "well done" will give you the high of a thousand lifetimes (Luke 19:17).

Will Jesus wear a crown? His crown is your crown, and you will reign with him (Revelation 20:6).

One day you'll take your buddies golfing on the icy rock formerly known as Planet Pluto. Just think how far your drive will go.

Self-Fulfilling Prophecies

If somebody whispers, "You're stupid," often enough, you'll begin to believe it. Once you believe it, you will think it. Like a radio jingle that won't go away, the "I am stupid" script gets stuck on a permanent loop. Once you believe it and think it, you might feel it. As the lie worms deeper into your heart, you'll feel stupid. Head hanging low, mind feeling dark, fear stinging your throat with vomit, you will, finally, act stupid.

The lies of the enemy create self-fulfilling prophecies.

The only way to unwind this self-defeating pattern is to tune in to a new whisper: *All that is true of Jesus is now true of you.* You must hear the whisper often, in different settings, when you succeed and when you fail. When you are happy and when you are sad. In every circumstance, trial, victory, or defeat, you must hear the echo of the Father's voice over and over again: You are complete in him (Colossians 2:10).

If that is good enough for God – and it is – then everybody who doubts it about you can go take a flying leap.

CHAPTER 6

Rehab

AUTHOR MALCOLM GLADWELL, in his powerful book, *Blink*, tells the story of an ancient Greek statue called the Kouros. Purchased for $7 million by the J. Paul Getty Museum, the Kouros depicts a naked youth, standing straight and tall at about six feet. The Kouros is remarkable for its completeness: head to toe intact, showing only minor blemishes.[3]

What made it valuable was its antiquity, dating from six centuries before Christ.

What made it a headache were suspicions of forgery that haven't gone away.

After fourteen months of scientific analysis using the most sophisticated technologies, the museum deemed the statue authentic and bought it. Gladwell then unfolds an increasing chorus of skepticism.

It started with an Italian art historian who, for reasons he couldn't articulate, felt uneasy over the fingernails. Evelyn Harrison, an expert on Greek sculpture, was next. Gladwell offers this interview with Harrison:

> [The curator] just swished a cloth off the top of it and said, "Well it isn't ours yet, but it will be in a couple of weeks." And I said, "I'm sorry to hear that." What did Harrison see? She didn't know. In that very first moment... all Harrison had was a hunch, an instinctive sense that something was amiss.[4]

The next scholar took one look and asked if the museum could get its money back. A later scholar described feeling "a wave of intuitive revulsion."[5]

What enabled these scholars to see in a flash what scientists couldn't see in fourteen months?

They had in their field what Christians might call *wisdom*.

Decades of academic study, combined with a wealth of experience, piled on top of a lifetime of reading, practice, and mentoring, produced a vast database of expertise in the field. When they saw the Kouros, their minds aggregated a lifetime of learning in a flash: they could spot a forgery even when electron microscopes could not.

They had so integrated deep truth into their lives that it was part of them – instinctive, intuitive, and fast. Gladwell subtitles his book "The Power of Thinking Without Thinking." What he means is that the logical processing happens so fast you can hardly see it – in a blink, as it were.

Such "thinking without thinking" is not for the uninitiated. A rookie paging through a handbook could never snap to decisions with such speed. It takes a lifetime of immersion into a field to develop the discernment that happens in the blink of an eye.

And so the Bible invites you to the epic adventure of renewing your mind.

> Be transformed by the renewing of your mind. (Romans 12:2)

And be renewed in the spirit of your mind. (Ephesians 4:23)

Therefore do not be unwise, but understand what the will of the Lord is. (Ephesians 5:17)

Create in me a clean heart, O God, / And renew a steadfast spirit within me. (Psalm 51:10)

Taking every thought into captivity to the obedience of Christ. (2 Corinthians 10:5)

When the devil hisses his disapproval, and the lunchroom bullies shout their curses, you need a chorus of voices to rise up within you and shout their lies into oblivion. You need to be so saturated with the truths of your identity in Christ that the devil can't stick in a crumb of self-loathing edgewise. You need to spot those self-deprecating labels in a blink, and vaporize them with a blast from your Scripture ray-gun.

And that Scripture needs to have been transplanted from the printed pages of a book, to the ethereal pages of your mind, heart, and soul.

Wisdom

Wisdom is the difference between dancing with reckless abandon (wisdom), versus counting steps on the dance-class floor (academic/immature knowledge only).

Wisdom is the difference between running bases with strategy and speed, versus needing a T-Ball coach to point the way.

Wisdom is the integration of divine truth into everyday thinking and feeling, so it becomes your second nature – your knee-jerk reaction in the blink of an eye.

Wisdom is thinking without thinking because you have thought long and hard on the thoughts of God in Scripture.

Only the mental renewal Scripture brings can arm you against the fiery darts of evil. Only this mental renewal – developed in secret, studied and prayed into your heart over time, illuminated and energized by God's Spirit – can confer upon you a divinely-birthed self-acceptance that withstands the harshest criticism from the nastiest boss, the crankiest father-in-law, the snippiest teenager, or the bluest-haired church lady. Only this mental renewal can unleash the power of your moral union with Christ.

That's why Part Two of this book serves up a feast of content-rich morsels about your true identity in Christ. It's time to begin renewing your mind.

Secret Weapons

The devil, the world, and the lunatics on your family tree conspire to compose self-loathing scripts for you. These scripts echo crazily in your mind: I'm a fat, stupid, worthless slob and nobody with half a brain would love me and I should die or at least cut myself. These scripts turn especially virulent when your imperfection shows. These scripts magnify your imperfection out of proportion. These voices are liars.

You need to listen to new voices.

Install new scripts.

Systematically create new structures of thinking, feeling, believing, knowing, and self-perceiving.

Wrestle your mind to stand on the Word of God against the clamor of a legion's lies.

In this fight, you are not alone. You can link arms with four allies. The Holy Spirit is your sponsor, the Word of God is your guide, a spiritual community is your friend, and consistency is the key.

1. The Holy Spirit

The Holy Spirit, God himself, steps forward as your mentor in this process. He energizes all your growth from behind the scenes. The Spirit convicts you when you embrace a lie, motivates you when you grow listless, and strengthens you to put one foot in front of the other when you feel you can't go on. He spots the devil's lies a mile away, and helps you put biblical crosshairs on the target. The Holy Spirit then blasts those lies into oblivion with a blow from his Mighty Sword, the Word of God (Ephesians 6:17).

I've had a rocky relationship with the Holy Spirit over the years. I've met super-spiritual people, who love God but freak me out. Some people associate the Spirit with dramatic manifestations like laughing or speaking in tongues. I admit, I have my shields up when it comes to those unusual works.

But I've come to believe this from Scripture: whatever I may feel or not feel, I can trust the Holy Spirit to work in his own gentle way. He isn't in the razzle-dazzle – the rushing wind, the flashing lightning, the earthquake – as much as in the "still small voice" (1 Kings 19:11,12, KJV). He works when I ask him to, even if I don't feel him. I just believe his promise to be there for me. I stand on his Word, and listen in the heat of the moment as the Spirit of Truth recalls to my mind the scriptural truths that I have. He makes real the things that have been freely given by God. He actualizes my potential in Christ.

Only the supernatural power of God's Spirit can untangle the knotted mess of lies I believe.

Only the Spirit can heal my broken heart, repair my damaged emotions, and undo a lifetime of radioactive decay from living in this broken world.

Only the Spirit can energize my union with Christ and actualize my true identity.

In a million years of striving, I could never imitate Christ by my own strength. But Christ can be himself through me by the power of his indwelling Spirit. My grace rehab will never run on human power alone. It requires God's power, and therefore is grace all the way. "'Not by might nor by power, but by My Spirit,' / Says the LORD" (Zechariah 4:6).

2. The Word of God

You will make no progress in biblical self-acceptance without regular immersion into the pages of the Holy Bible. There is no substitute for the Word of God. Daily devotions. Daily Bible reading. Chewing on Scripture's words and sentences and phrases.

The Bible is the supernatural therapist for you mental and emotional renewal.

Without the Bible, you cannot trust your impressions. Without the Bible to guide you, you cannot trust your way. Feelings will lie to you. Mental impressions will be out of phase. The voices in your head will too often sing the devil's tune.

Unless you wrangle every mental whisper to its rightful submission under the authority of the written Word of God, you'll be a sucker for forgeries. Why were the experts able to pick out the false Kouros? Because they had installed a massive database of antiquities-facts into their heart of hearts. As soon as they saw the fake, their inner spirit compiled the data in a flash, and they knew.

For the Christian, the Bible supplies that database. Doctrines. Promises. Truths. Commands. A revelation of the heart of God. The Bible creates in you a plumb line to measure every truth-claim.

But what the Bible brings to you goes beyond simple data. When you spend time in God's Word, you're not just taking in information, you're also taking in power. The living and powerful Word of God sinks into your soul to radiate transforming truth in your inmost being: "Behold, You desire truth in the inward parts, / And in the hidden *part* You will make me to know wisdom" (Psalm 51:6).

Our grandparents' generation wore out their leather Bibles.

Now it's our turn.

My friend, Tim, told me how every morning of his childhood, he'd come downstairs to get ready for school, and he would see his dad's open Bible on the kitchen table. His dad had already gone to work, but Tim knew how his dad's day had started.

> For though by this time you ought to be teachers, you need someone to teach you again the first principles of the oracles of God; and you have come to need milk and not solid food. For everyone who partakes only of milk is unskilled in the word of righteousness, for he is a babe. But solid food belongs to those who are of full age, that is, those who by reason of use have their senses exercised to discern both good and evil. (Hebrews 5:12-14)

It is God's Word, installed into your deepest thinking, that gives you discernment between good and evil, truth and error, the devil's lies and God's reality.

Nothing in this book will work for you, and you will never overcome the deeply ingrained scripts of the past, without a regular diet of God's Word. In Part Two, you'll find a running start, with daily Bible studies to get you going.

3. Church

You need a good church. A good church: a) has lots of imperfect people, so you can fit in; b) offers music that speaks your language; c) preaches sermons from the Bible with integrity, authenticity, and grace – sermons that don't beat you up; and, d) has small groups. Or Sunday School classes. Or Life Groups. Or some kind of human-sized groups for you to join.

That way, someone has your back.

That way, life doesn't feel so lonely.

Like having a running partner, or a friend in the kitchen to mince the garlic while you chop the greens.

God is a Trinity: three persons in one Godhead. That means God doesn't experience his existence alone – the Father loves the Son who loves the Spirit who loves the Father.

When he created you, he wove a drive for connection into you. You might be an introvert, like me, preferring a handful of deep friendships over dozens of shallow ones. That's fine.

Or you might be the life of the party – a confirmed extrovert – who thrives on people and parties and "working the room."

Either way, God insists that his people act like a [functional] family.

Keep shopping till you find a church that speaks your language. No fake excuses that they're all a bunch of hypocrites, or that whatever. Get your rear end into a good church. Throw on some clothes, brush your teeth, and drag yourself to church. And plug way in.

Somebody has to pat you on the back when you deserve it.

Or whack you upside the head (lovingly, figuratively, not literally) when you need it – mainly by pointing out the self-defeating lies you believe.

A good church will give you both.

> And let us not neglect our meeting together, as some people do, but encourage and warn each other,

especially now that the day of his coming back again
is drawing near. (Hebrews 10:25, NLT)

One warning: if a church feels creepy or cultlike or harsh and judgmental, keep shopping. Life's too short to needlessly expose yourself to the rancid stench of self-righteous Pharisees.

4. Consistency

I've been a pastor for a long time – how long would require I disclose my age, which isn't about to happen. Let's just say it has been long enough for me to observe a singular problem that derails the spiritual development of more Christians than any other problem. Are you ready for this mother of all spiritual dysfunctions?

It is *intermittent motivation.* It is being sporadic with God.

You are on fire for God, involved in Bible study and prayer and small groups and service. This lasts for two and a half years. Then bad stuff happens. An illness. A messy divorce. Disco makes a comeback.

This trial makes you mad at God. So you're out. Bye-bye church. Bye-bye Bible. Bye-bye prayer, worship, fellowship. Bye-bye God. He gets the cold shoulder. Over time, your disappointment with God festers, like a pus-filled wound. Left untended, it becomes your all-purpose hall pass to either, a) a long roster of sins you thought you'd never commit, or, b) a lifestyle contentedly independent of God.

Some time later, the convicting power of the Holy Spirit breaks through, and you regret the departure. So you haul your tearful self back to church. Plug back in. Get moving again.

Until the next disappointment with God... and you're out again.

You cannot flip the switch on and off over and over again without stalling your spiritual maturity. You will never develop wisdom. You'll never develop the momentum you need to blast through life's inevitable difficulties.

You need to stay the course.

You need to stay consistent with God over the long haul.

You need to quit yanking up your fragile roots only to start over a year later. Stay put in church, with God, the Bible, prayer, and community, and let those roots grow strong and deep. Don't let adversity drive a wedge between you and God. Don't hand Satan that kind of victory. You claim your identity by renewing your mind – integrating truth into your deepest thinking, feeling, and believing. It's walking with God through your toughest times that kicks that renewal into overdrive.

And it's consistency over time that enables you to keep walking through life's inevitable storms.

5. All of the above

The Bible tells a great story when one of God's best people is ready to call it quits. Elijah held the title as Ultimate Fighter for God in his generation. Right after his greatest achievement, he found himself worn out, depressed, and ready to call it quits on God and on life.

> But [Elijah] went a day's journey into the wilderness, and came and sat down under a broom tree. And he prayed that he might die, and said, "It is enough! Now, LORD, take my life, for I am no better than my fathers!" (1 Kings 19:4)

What do you think God gave him first? A Bible study? A prayer time? A holy zap of revelation knowledge? A spiritual manifestation of glory? A vision of heaven?

No.

God gave him a nap.

And God gave him a few good meals.

Depressed Elijah found so much strength, in the next scene he runs 40 days and nights to his next mission from God (1 Kings 19:4-8).

God made you a body, soul, and spirit – one person, three parts, intricately connected. Some of your spiritual problems can have physical roots. Or soulish – psychological – roots. Or spiritual, God-related roots.

That's why I encourage you to adopt an all-of-the-above approach to healing the deep needs of your life. Take care of your physical needs through nutrition, rest, sound medical care, and exercise.

Take care of your psychological needs through family, friends, recreation, vacations, and maybe even counseling. Many churches have several layers of counseling: volunteer, pastoral, or professional. Everybody needs help, once in a while. Don't be too proud.

And nourish your spirit through Scripture, prayer, and church.

All of the above.

You can learn all of your riches in Christ, and, like Elijah, still feel poor if you're worn out or malnourished.

Rehab

You need rehab. You can't live like Christ unless you think like Christ. You can't express *your truest, deepest self,* unless you follow his steps. Jesus, the Bible says, grew "in wisdom and stature," and so must you (Luke 2:52).

The Bible exhorts you to "take every thought captive," "be renewed in the spirit of your mind," "be transformed by the renewing of your mind," and "lay hold of that for which Christ laid hold of you" (2 Corinthians 10:5, Ephesians 4:23, Romans 12:2, Philippians 3:12).

It's not enough to claim your identity as a kind of "positive thinking" or "name it and claim it" technique. You need an entire rewiring of your mental and emotional circuitry (also called *repentance*), in order to make your new sense of self stable.

Let's work on that now.

In each of the following chapters, you will find a central biblical truth about your identity in Christ.

God gave you these truths to heal you. He gave them to equip you for the life of your dreams, and to bring to maturity within you a triumphant spirit. Here you will find a voice louder than the bullies of your past, stronger than the hissing disapproval of your dysfunctional family, and truer than any deceptions the dark lord has snuck into your spirit.

You are in union with Christ. Now, let's learn to think that way, so you can live that way.

PART TWO
In Christ, I Am...

CHAPTER 7

I AM FORGIVEN

Meditation

We are now pardoned; even now are our sins put away; even now we stand in the sight of God accepted, as though we had never been guilty. "There is therefore now no condemnation to them which are in Christ Jesus." There is not a sin in the Book of God, even now, against one of His people. ~Charles H. Spurgeon, 1800s

Scripture

"Come now, and let us reason together," Says the LORD, "Though your sins are like scarlet, They shall be as white as snow; Though they are red like crimson, They shall be as wool. (Isaiah 1:18)

Bible Study

THIS CHAPTER ON FORGIVENESS is written by a guy whose middle name is "guilt trip." The little church that reared me blessed me beyond words; I'm thankful for that. But I'm also recovering from the painful labels of unworthiness and guilt slapped on me during those formative years.

Sometimes a church can feel like a travel agent for a guilt trip.

No matter how many prayers I prayed or good works I squeezed out, I was sure God was judging me for my

71

sins. I cringed to think of standing in his presence. Even though I was saved, I still stooped beneath a hundred pound sack of guilt.

So I did what any self-respecting church kid would do: I made myself super-busy for Jesus. I served him all the time. If the church doors were open, I was there. But my service wasn't out of love; it was out of guilt. I didn't know it at the time, but my service was a form of penance, and I didn't even believe in penance.

Today, I can say with all belief that I am permanently, profoundly, and perfectly forgiven by God forever. This is not because God is wimpy, but because the Cross of Christ is strong.

What made the difference?

An understanding of the Cross and what happened for me the day Jesus died.

A Forgiving God

The astounding announcement of the prophets and apostles of old is the good news of a forgiving God.

In Christ, you stand fully, completely, perfectly, everlastingly forgiven of all your sins, past, present and future. Even if you went out and invented a brand new sin – a big, juicy, heinous sin no one had ever done before – your forgiveness from God wouldn't even flicker.

This is not due to God's leniency, softness, niceness, or "unconditional" love. To reduce the biblically glorious wonder of forgiveness into a divine wimpiness, by which the Creator winks at sin, is to set yourself up for a lifetime of a troubled conscience.

We need a forgiveness that means something – a forgiveness so strong that a thousand shouts of devilish accusation can't shake it. And that is exactly what God has lavished upon us, courtesy the Cross of Christ.

A Holy God

Behind the Cross lies the initially uncomfortable, but ultimately beautiful, reality of an infinitely holy God. If God were not holy, Jesus would not have died.

The holiness of God implies two very scary truths for any thinking person:

The first is that sinful people cannot dwell in God's presence. If God is holy, anyone who has sinned stands alienated from him. In other words, if God is holy, you can't be his friend without measuring up to his standards. So the Bible says we are "alienated from the life of God," and, we were "alienated and enemies" of God "by wicked works" (Ephesians 4:18, Colossians 1:21).

This is horrible news.

But wait, there's more, and the second truth is worse:

God's holiness also implies that sinful people fall under condemnation from the justice of God. It's not just that we're alienated from God; as sinners we're condemned by God, too. I know this feeds into a lot of negative stereotypes about God, but we do ourselves no favors by avoiding the difficult truth. God judges sin. The Bible says, "the wrath of God is revealed from heaven against all ungodliness and unrighteousness" of people (Romans 1:18). Jesus warned anyone who stood aloof from his way of forgiveness that "the wrath of God abides on him" (John 3:36). This wrath lasts forever (Matthew 25:46).

Far from being a grandmotherly leniency on the part of a God too wimpy to care, true forgiveness can be nothing less than a tough, rigorous, righteous action on the part of a frighteningly holy God.

The Non-Dilemma

"God is love," says John (1 John 4:8).

"Our God is a consuming fire," says Hebrews (12:29).

Do you see a problem here? God's love won't bless where his holiness is offended. From our standpoint, this looks like a dilemma. God, however, is too smart to ever have a dilemma. In his perfect plan, he made a way to love us without tossing his holiness into the dumpster.

Enter the Cross, where Jesus died. The crucifixion towers above history as a monument to both the fierce wrath and invincible love of God. Take away either, and the Cross makes no sense.

When Christ was nailed to the cross, your sins were nailed to Christ. This is the lesson God had to teach me to deliver me from my load of guilt. I'll never forget the day. I sat in my musty high school gymnasium – in the same school that so tormented Susan – reading a book about the cross of Christ. Suddenly, the lights came on. I got it. It clicked. The Cross made sense to me. And that hundred pound sack of guilt dropped to the ground. In an instant I knew I was forgiven.

My sins were nailed to Christ, and he paid the price for them. Your sins were nailed to Christ and paid for too.

God reached into you – long before you were born – and collected all your sins. Every failure, every loss, every hatred, every lie, every immoral thought, every abuse, cruelty, and omission – every sin, past, present and future, God collected them all.

He then transferred your sins to Christ.

So the Bible says, Jesus "himself bore our sins in his own body" on the cross (1 Peter 2:24). "The Lord [God the Father] laid on him [God the Son] the iniquity of us all," said Isaiah (Isaiah 53:6).

In the language of theology, God *imputed* your sins to Christ, along with all their guilt and shame. Christ hung on that cross as if he had done your crimes, committed your sins, and failed your failures.

Then God did the unthinkable: he punished Christ for your sins instead of punishing you. The pent up Judgment Day against a world gone wild was unleashed against the bloodied Savior, hanging all alone, between heaven and earth. "Christ crucified" was the lightning rod that absorbed God's wrath that he might spare you. He died as your substitute.

He died horribly. Painfully. In utter agony. Forsaken and alone. We bow in humble adoration at the bloody crucifixion of our precious Savior.

Because of that death, God is free to dismiss your sins from his presence. He sees no guilt in you – you stand faultless before him (Jude 24).

Because of what Christ did.

Not because of what you did. No, not even a tiny bit.

Don't you think Christ's sacrifice was enough? Is there anything you can add? Are there coins you might supply to sweeten the deal with God? Did Jesus accidentally leave a few sins behind for you to atone for?

Crazy-talk.

In his final breath, Jesus said, "It is finished" (John 19:30) – the best words ever uttered on planet earth. The payment for your sin was finished. The judgment of God against you was finished. Your guilt and shame were finished, once for all, on the cross, by Christ alone.

"Behold, the Lamb of God, who takes away the sin of the world" (John 1:29).

That is why you can say today, *I am forgiven* – totally, irrevocably, everlastingly, forgiven – for all my sins, past, present, and future. You possess a hard-fought, blood-bought, paid in full, comprehensive, once for all, perfectly legitimized, unassailable forgiveness from the heart of your magnificently holy God. You did not deserve it. You did not earn it. You can't contribute to it. You received it the day God joined you to Christ.

If you've never been saved, you can be saved right now. You can tell God you are believing in Jesus as your Savior. Set aside this book, and tell him you are trusting in Christ, crucified and risen again, as your only hope for eternal forgiveness. There are no magic words, just ask him to save you by faith alone in Christ alone, and he will. He will give you the free gift of eternal life and he will join you to Christ forever.

In Christ, God labels you FORGIVEN. He longs for you to label yourself FORGIVEN too.

Additional Scriptures

Psalm 103:10-12, Romans 8:1, Ephesians 1:7, John 8:1-11.

Prayer

Dear Lord,

I stand today in the forgiveness purchased by Jesus Christ on the cross. Thank you for such a sacrifice. By the Cross, you honored both your holiness and your love. Your forgiveness of me is just, holy, righteous, and pure. I stand free from guilt, free from shame, free from condemnation.

Thank you, God, for the Cross of Christ. Thank you for Calvary Love. I am humbled and grateful when I think of that great sacrifice. Such agony, such pain, such a death, for me. I bless you as my Savior. I worship you as my King. I find my shelter in the shadow of the cross, and know no sin can condemn me there.

I claim my forgiveness in Christ, today and everyday.

On the authority if Christ's Cross, I label myself FORGIVEN.

I may fail a thousand times today. I may let you down. I may let myself down.

But of this I am sure: you have forgiven me, once for all. You have cast my sins behind your back and dismissed them as far as the east is from the west. You have washed me in the blood of the Lamb.

I peel off the labels of guilt and shame. I peel off the labels of self-punishment. I peel off labels of penance. I rest my conscience at the foot of the cross. I tell the accusing voices in my head that your forgiveness of me is total, permanent, finished, and exhaustive. I command those voices to be silent. God has spoken. I am clean. I am forgiven. It is finished.

The only label I accept today when it comes to my sins is FORGIVEN.

Today, dear Father, help me walk in the light of your perfect forgiveness. And help me extend the same hand of mercy to those who offend me.

Through My Precious Savior I pray.

Amen.

CHAPTER 8

I AM JUSTIFIED

Meditation

How dangerous it is to join anything of our own to the righteousness of Christ, in pursuit of justification before God! Jesus Christ will never endure this; it reflects upon His work dishonorably. He will be all, or none, in our justification. If He has finished the work, what need is there of our additions? And if not, to what purpose are they? Can we finish that which Christ Himself could not complete? Did He finish the work, and will He ever divide the glory and praise of it with us? No, no; Christ is no half-Savior. It is a hard thing to bring proud hearts to rest upon Christ for righteousness. God humbles the proud by calling sinners wholly from their own righteousness to Christ for their justification. ~John Flavel, 1600s

Scripture

Therefore, having been justified by faith, we have peace with God through our Lord Jesus Christ. (Romans 5:1)

Bible Study

YOU CAN THINK OF FORGIVENESS as subtraction and justification as addition. Imagine digging a hole a hundred feet deep and being stuck inside. The hole represents your sins. Through *forgiveness*, God lifted you out of the hole, set you on solid ground, and filled the hole so well you could never tell it existed. You were lifted upward from negative-100 all the way to ground zero.

But that is not enough. It is not enough for God to simply subtract your sins.

You'd still be missing something: you'd be missing the righteousness which God requires for those who would stand in his presence.

Don't let the word "righteousness" intimidate you. It simply means *goodness that's good enough for God.* Look at it this way: when God forgave you, he subtracted the badness; when he justified you, he added the goodness. All of this happened in a flash at the very first instant you were saved.

Jesus frequently pounded the cocky little heads of religious people called Pharisees. The Pharisees were famous for their observance of God's laws. They prayed and went to church and tithed and did all kinds of favors for God. Nobody could touch them in the righteousness department.

Or so it seemed.

One day, Jesus freaked everybody out when he said,

> For I say to you, that unless your righteousness exceeds the righteousness of the scribes and Pharisees, you will by no means enter the kingdom of heaven. (Matthew 5:20)

He pointed to the most over-the-top "righteous" people of his day, and said, "Not enough."

I don't think the Pharisees liked hearing that. I imagine a gasp big enough to suck the oxygen out of the room.

Not Enough

Your human-energized righteousness will never be good enough for God. No matter how sincere, how genuine, how sacrificial, or how religious. You still fall short. Your best endeavors still merit Christ's judgment.

Logic says so. How can finite, limited goodness ever qualify for the approval of Infinite Holiness?

Nature also says so. The Old Testament says so. The New Testament says so. The prophets and apostles said so. Jesus said so. And, if you quit boasting long enough to shut your mouth, and listen hard, you'll hear that your own conscience says so.

All these voices bear witness to an eternal truth: you'll never be good enough for God in your own power and strength. All these voices say so because God says so, and he says so because it's reality.

By any standard of justice, the courts of heaven and the Heavenly Judge had no choice but to condemn you, and to banish you – the unrighteous person – from the face of the Divine Judge forever.

Enter the most sparkly treasure in the Christian's treasury.

God is Enough

Into your insufficiency, God pours his sufficiency. Over your unrighteousness, God slathers his own righteousness like peanut butter on bread.

> [That I may be] found in Him, not having my own righteousness, which is from the law, but that which is through faith in Christ, the righteousness which is from God by faith. (Philippians 3:9)

The righteousness of Christ shines brightly enough to dazzle the angels forever. It most certainly meets the approval of the Heavenly Father. And the astounding news of the gospel is that you've become a full partner in that righteousness. God has deposited an immeasurable quantity of his own righteousness into your heavenly account. What an awesome gift!

This was the very commodity you needed most:

Righteousness to erase the guilt of your most embarrassing secrets.

Righteousness to counteract the weight of dysfunction in your soul.

Righteousness to clear your record of guilt.

Righteousness to fill you with goodness that is good enough for God.

Righteousness to satisfy all God's demands of you.

Righteousness to put you on par with the righteousness of Christ, because it *is* the righteousness of Christ.

Righteousness to silence those pesky voices telling you you'll never be good enough.

Righteousness to make you feel accepted, acceptable, worthy, valued, treasured, cherished, beloved, and beautiful to God and his court.

Like a radiant garment, shimmering with glory, you have been robed in the righteousness of God. I love this beautiful exclamation of the ancient prophet Isaiah:

> I am overwhelmed with joy in the LORD my God! For he has dressed me with the clothing of salvation and draped me in a robe of righteousness... (Isaiah 61:10, NLT)

When you received Christ, you received Christ's righteousness too. This righteousness changes everything important about you.

It changes your identity: you became a whole new person when you received it.

It changes your privileges: your righteousness brings with it rights and powers you never had before.

It changes your access: the righteousness of God becomes your all-access pass to the heavenly realms, not only in eternity, but in time, right now, on this planet's school of hard knocks.

It changes your nature: you're no longer defined by your problems, addictions, and hang-ups; God's righteousness means you're bigger than all of them and those issues are increasingly defined by you.

It changes your status before God: You were guilty, you become pardoned. You were alienated, you become reconciled. You were condemned, you become justified. You were a child of wrath, you become a child of God.

Of all the treasures in the Christian's treasury, the first, and most precious, is the righteousness of God.

I'm spending time on this gift of righteousness, because it becomes the landing pad for every other blessing in your life. God blesses righteousness wherever he sees it. But you have none of your own that measures up. So God gives you Christ's own righteousness, looks down and declares you righteous, and then starts firing down every other blessing you can conceive. Has there ever been good news as good news-ish as this?

What Does Justified Mean?

If you are a Christian, God says you are "justified freely by his grace" (Romans 3:24a). What does it mean to be justified?

To be justified means to be looked at by God, scrutinized by God, put under God's microscope, studied under the blazing gaze of divine holiness, morally x-rayed inside and out, examined, inspected, reviewed, and analyzed before the eyes of him to whom all things are laid bare – and then to have that same, all-knowing God, declare that you have passed inspection with flying colors.

On the day you were saved, God justified you. On the day he justified you, he declared you to be fully and perfectly righteous before the courts of heaven forever and ever through all the ages long.

Justification is the act of God in declaring the believing sinner to be righteous, based, not upon the sinner's righteousness, but upon the righteousness of God given the moment you first believed.

This is not a righteousness of *behavior* – you still might be a jerk.

This is a righteousness of *status* – the great gift deposited into your heavenly accounts, making you rich by someone else's wealth.

So What?

You've probably already experienced a painful reality: the moment you cease resting in Christ's righteousness, you begin working to establish your own. Christians who don't feel righteous feel anxious. They feel a need to prove something.

And they're brittle. They're always justifying themselves, and arguing with the air why the other person is wrong, even if that person is a million miles away. Or dead.

So they feel tired. Christianity wears them out.

Do you know how you know when justification has taken root in your mind and heart and soul?

When you rest in the finished work of Christ.

When you live with nothing left to prove.

When you let bullets of accusation bounce off your superhero chest.

When you accept God's acceptance of you.

When the lag time between guilt and grace keeps growing shorter.

When you spend less time in the kitchen (Martha) making dry sandwiches for Heaven's Chef (Jesus) and more time in the living room (Mary), feasting on the riches of what he's brought to the table.

You.

Are.

Righteous.

Bank on it.

Additional Scriptures

Romans 5:1, 1 Corinthians 6:11, Genesis 15:6, Romans 4:3.

Prayer

My Gracious Father,

How I praise you for this stupendous gift of divine righteousness. I take my stand today in the great gift of justification, full and free. I declare that, in Christ, I am righteous. You've shouted my declaration of righteousness before angels and demons, heaven, hell, and the devil, in a voice to echo through the cosmos for all the ages long.

I am good enough for you, God, no matter what the accusing voices may say.

I am righteous in your sight, no matter what others may see in me.

I am qualified for the blessings of heaven, no matter who might disqualify me on earth.

I confess I have no merit of my own. None. No righteousness to prevail before the heavenly courts. No goodness to withstand your blistering judgment. Nothing to warrant even the slightest smile from you, except that which you have given me.

Sometimes I wonder what you see in me. Today, I remind myself that you see your own sparkling righteousness in me, radiating the joy and goodness of heaven.

My old labels said, "Unworthy. Undesirable. Ugly."

My new labels – those glimmering gifts of grace – declare me "Worthy. Desired. Beautiful."

On the authority of your Word, I label myself JUSTIFIED.

I declare that what you see in me is true: I've been justified, and will be forever. Help me Lord, to rest my anxious heart in my exalted status before you. And help me to look beyond the surface of those I rub shoulders with today, that I may begin to see the beauty you see in them too.

Through my Savior, Jesus, I pray,

Amen.

CHAPTER 9

I AM RECONCILED

Meditation

All that is necessary to our reconciliation — Jesus has done, Jesus has suffered; and looking to him, and resting on what he has done — we may be on terms of peace with a righteous and holy God, at any moment. But peace can only be obtained at the cross. Cross of Jesus! You are the foundation of my hope, the ground of my confidence, the source of my comfort, and my daily boast... Nothing will calm a troubled conscience, nothing will silence an accusing devil, nothing will allay the fears of the heart, nothing will smooth the dying pillow — but the blood of the cross. ~James Smith, 1860

Scripture

And you, who once were alienated and enemies in your mind by wicked works, yet now He has reconciled in the body of His flesh through death, to present you holy, and blameless, and above reproach in His sight. (Colossians 1:21, 22)

I will arise and go to my father, and will say to him, "Father, I have sinned against heaven and before you, and I am no longer worthy to be called your son. Make me like one of your hired servants." And he arose and came to his father. But when he was still a great way off, his father saw him and had compassion, and ran and fell on his neck and kissed him. (Luke 15:18-20)

Bible Study

SWEAT SLICKED HIS PALMS, and his mind raced. *Stupid! Stupid! Get it right!* he told himself. One foot landed in front of the other on the dirty road leading home. The smells and sounds of the city receded behind him. The open road offered no comfort.

With every footfall, he felt a hard fist reach up from his guts and tighten its hold on his throat.

"Dad... uh... Father, Sir, I screwed up..." He rehearsed his speech out loud. Shifted his threadbare backpack. Kept trudging forward. Dust swirled in little eddies around his feet. He had one shot. Just one shot to get it right. Everything depended on it. If his pitch weren't perfect, they'd find his rotted carcass beside some lonely road. He knew it.

No. Say *Father*, not *Dad*. Don't say *Sir*. And not *screwed up*... he's too old for that.

"Father, I have sinned against you."

Yeah. Keep that. No wait. It's more than that. I really screwed things up with God...The shame almost made him cry. My dad needs to know I know that...

"Father, I have sinned against heaven..."

Not enough...

"Father, I have sinned against heaven and in your sight..."

A grimy hand wiped sweat from his brow. He pushed back depressing memories of sleazy nights and shameful days. Choked back vomit. Such a fool... one foot plodded in front of the other, and increasing dread broke through the numbness with each step.

God Is Not Mad At You

God is not mad at you. Isn't hacked off. He doesn't sit in heaven shaking his head in disappointment at you. God could no more be angry at you than he could be angry at Christ. Christ is your identity, and in him, God is well-pleased.

Jesus told a story the world calls The Prodigal Son (Luke 15:11-32). Though Jesus never used the word "prodigal," it fits. Prodigal means out of bounds. Past the limits. Over the top. A perfect description of this twisted, stoned out, greedy little S.O.B. (Son of Belial).

Jesus made him as bad as he could, to create in us as much hope as he could. If a Father so good could reconcile to himself a child so bad, then maybe there's hope for me. That's the idea.

Before the son reached home, his father saw him from afar, Jesus said. The son alienated himself from the Father, but the Father never stopped longing for his embrace. He never stopped watching at the head of the road, waiting for his son to come home.

That is how your Father in heaven feels toward you every single day.

To reconcile means to restore the relationship between warring parties. Reconciliation brings hostilities to a close.

What hostilities?

Like a nasty divorce, sin fractured mankind's relationship with God. The fracture was all on our part. God never left us, we left him, and slammed the door on the way out. Scripture says we were "alienated and enemies in [our] minds by [our] wicked works" (Colossians 1:21). We were "alienated from the life of God" (Ephesians 4:18). Our iniquities have "separated between" us and God; and our sins have "hidden his face" from us (Isaiah 59:2).

In other words, your sinfulness represented the moral equivalent of you grabbing a fistful of credit cards from Dad's wallet, running out the door, flipping him the bird on the way out, and partying your life away in self-destructive insanity. That insanity may have been reckless, like the prodigal son's. Or it may have been polished and diligent, like the elder brother's (Luke 15:25-32). The fact remains: your pre-saved self was alienated from God by choice, by nature, and by status.

No amount of praying, paying, fasting, serving, repenting, atoning, sacrificing, new-leaf-turning, or good-works-doing could repair the breach between you and God.

Enter the love of the Father and the Cross of Christ. He has reconciled you "in the body of His flesh through death" (Colossians 1:21). Once again, the Ground Zero of all good things is Christ and his Cross. By him, the breach is repaired. The gap is closed. The war is over. Hostilities ceased. This is the beauty of reconciliation.

At Christmastime we sing:

Peace on earth, and mercy mild,

God and sinners reconciled!

That is the power of the Cross of Christ. Your reconciliation is entirely the work of God. Not one bit of its weight rests on your wimpy shoulders. Jesus paid it all.

Reconciled by Grace

You don't reconcile yourself to God; he reconciled you back to himself.

You don't reconcile God to yourself; you are the object of reconciliation and God is the subject. In other words, God never needed reconciliation; you did. God was always standing at the head of the road, waiting for you to come home. God was always ready to run to you, hug you, shower you with kisses, and throw a feast for your return.

God was ready for you long before you were ready for him.

The alienation was all your doing.

The reconciliation was all God's doing.

And now, all that remains is for you to enjoy your Father's love every single day. You are reconciled on good days and bad days. Reconciled whether you pray or don't pray. Serve or don't serve. Bear fruit or lie fallow.

You can't lose your reconciliation. Can't fracture it, rupture it, soil it. You may lose the joy of it, but that's easy to fix.

You are in Christ, remember? Can you imagine the harmonies of heaven as the Father, Son, and Holy Spirit sing out divine love? Not a hint of dissonance. Not a whiff off key. And by the beautiful doctrine of reconciliation, you've been brought into that eternal harmony. Even on your very worst days – on your most shameful days as a child of God – if you can muster the faith to join the chorus, heaven's glory will swell with greater praise because Christ himself sings through you. And, in him, you just can't sing off key.

You never have to massage your relationship with God. You've been reconciled to him, and the glue is stronger than atomic fusion. You never have to prepare a speech to pacify him. No grandiose gestures needed. No sacrifices. No offerings. No promises to do better next time.

Just come home.

Have you sinned again?

Have you blown it mightily? Embarrassingly? Repeatedly?

Come back and enjoy your fellowship again.

If you think you have to grovel to get a hug from God, you've got the wrong label on him. And on yourself. The elixir of reconciliation has not seeped into your psyche.

Say it out loud: I AM RECONCILED!

Life with God is a feast. There's a seat at the table set for you.

Dinner is served.

For Christ's sake, just sit down and dine already.

Additional Scriptures

Romans 5:11, 2 Corinthians 5:18, 2 Corinthians 5:20.

Prayer

Loving Father,

May the anxieties I feel about you melt away before the warmth of reconciliation. You've welcomed me home. You've wrapped me up. You've set the table for me. By faith, I join the banquet today, and feast on the riches of grace.

Whatever hostilities existed between us have been washed away forever. Whatever stresses existed between us are all on my side alone. You reached out to me with a hand of peace. Of blessing. You've never withdrawn that hand; you wait for me to take it. So today, I take it.

Whatever else I have to worry about today, I will not worry about "us." I have been reconciled to you by the blood of your Son; on my very worst day, not even the devil on steroids could alienate me from you.

I reject labels of rejection. I accept your acceptance of me.

I draw close to you emotionally because I am close to you in reality.

A thousand stresses may drop on my head today, but here is my peace: I will not stress about how you feel about me. The war is over, hostility has ceased, and heaven's harmonies resound through me.

You label me RECONCILED, so reconciled I am.

I will live this day with the easy confidence of a friend of the One in charge.

Let my reconciliation with you spill over into reconciliation with those around me. As far as possible from my side, help me live at peace with everyone.

By faith, I rise up today into my privilege as a "minister of reconciliation." Help me point somebody who's hurting to your loving embrace today.

In Christ I pray,

Amen.

CHAPTER 10

I AM ADOPTED

Meditation

Adoption is that act of God, whereby those were by nature the children of wrath, even as others, and were of the lost and ruined family of Adam, are from no reason in themselves, but entirely of the pure grace of God, translated out of the evil family of Satan, and brought actually and vitally into the family of God; so that they take his name, share the privileges of sons and they are to all intents and purposes the actual offspring and children of God. ~Charles H. Spurgeon, 1800s

Scripture

For you did not receive the spirit of bondage again to fear, but you received the Spirit of adoption by whom we cry out, "Abba, Father." (Romans 8:15)

Bible Study

YOUR UNION WITH CHRIST joined you to the family of God – you share Christ's wonderful family status as a child of God. You are his son or daughter in faith's bloodline.

You may have grown up in a wildly dysfunctional family. Insanity, like fleas, hopped from person to person in your crazy family tree. You may look back on a long line of addicts, criminals, and abusers. Snooty religionists. Arrogant rebels.

No matter what your family of origin was like, God has given you a new family. Yes, we all bring our dysfunctions to the table, but the Father's wholesomeness is more than enough to counteract your kinfolk's craziness. Your Heavenly Father easily delivers his finest blessings behind the iron curtain of earthly dysfunction.

In what many would find the most meaningful reality ever uttered about God, the Bible calls him "a father of the fatherless" (Psalm 68:5). God promises to fill in the gaps left by our imperfect earthly parents. Emotional gaps. Spiritual gaps. Even physical and financial gaps. God will move heaven and earth to prove to you that "father" is a verb, as he works tirelessly to unravel the painful knots tied by the failings of your earthly parents.

Adoption in ancient Roman society was not exactly the same as adoption today. A son born into a wealthy Roman family grew up without rights. He shared the same legal status as the household's slaves. He was not an heir simply by birth, and he had no legal standing in the family.

When the boy turned thirteen, the father vested him with the legal rights of an adult son. There was a ceremony for this, like a christening or a baptism. The son by birth was made son by status. For the first time, he enjoyed all the legal rights of being his Father's son. He was no longer a slave, but a son.

Perhaps Paul had something like this in mind when he wrote, "Therefore you are no longer a slave but a son, and if a son, then an heir of God through Christ" (Galatians 4:7).

Being a child of God is a mind-blowing privilege. Your dad is the richest dad of all. No earthly parent is more loving, generous, powerful, and kind.

God is your Father in the best, most ideal sense possible. Whatever crud has accumulated over your father-concept – maybe your dad let you down or even hurt you – does not apply to God. Not even one little bit. Your truest Father loves you with a perfect love. You are the apple of his eye. He delights to call you his own.

God invites you to call him "Abba," which means Daddy.

He is a Father who provides for you. "Or what man is there among you who, if his son asks for bread, will give him a stone?" (Matthew 7:9).

He is a Father who protects you. "He shall cover you with His feathers, / And under His wings you shall take refuge; / His truth shall be your shield and buckler" (Psalm 91:4).

He is a Father who notices you. "But the very hairs of your head are all numbered" (Matthew 10:30).

He is a Father who exalts you – he wears out the angels bragging about how awesome you are. "For to which of the angels did He ever say: 'You are My Son, Today I have begotten You'?" (Hebrews 1:5).

He is a Father who stays with you – abandonment is not in his vocabulary. "...He will be with you, He will not leave you nor forsake you; do not fear nor be dismayed" (Deuteronomy 31:8).

He is a Father who glorifies you. Your whole life story traces His plan to heap an avalanche of honor, glory, and celestial blessings on you some day. He is "bringing many sons [and daughters] to glory" (Hebrews 2:10).

You have been placed as an adult son or daughter into the royal family of God. His love for you equals his love for Christ. He approves of you. No frown of criticism ever creases his face. He looks upon you with joy. His name is your name. His wealth is your wealth. And his love is your love.

Your Father delights in you, and can hardly wait to welcome you home.

Additional Scriptures

Proverbs 3:12, Galatians 4:5-7, John 1:12, Galatians 3:26.

Prayer

My Gracious Father,
How I thank you for that glorious day you adopted me into your forever family. I was like an abandoned orphan wandering the streets, but you sought me out, and wrapped me up in your loving embrace. You made me your child forever.
Father. Abba. Daddy. I climb into your lap today. I rest in your love. I take my stand in the rights and privileges as a royal child of the Living God.
I calm my anxious heart in the knowledge of your ceaseless care. I profess to all the world your marvelous provision and presence.

I confess you as a father of the fatherless. I bless your name for the faithful ways you are filling up the gaps and healing the painful wounds left by my imperfect earthly parents. Lord, no matter how dysfunctional my earthly family has been, you have brought me into the most wholesome, whole, beautiful, and joyful family the cosmos has ever known.

Dad, take my hand, please, and walk me safely across this busy street called life-in-a-fallen-world. I'm already hungry for that glorious, raucous, joyful family dinner we will share someday in heaven's kitchen.

Until that day, grant me kindness and love for my brothers and sisters in the family of faith, and for all people.

Through Jesus,

Amen.

CHAPTER 11

I AM ACCEPTED

Meditation

When God accepts a sinner, He is, in fact, only accepting Christ. He looks into the sinner's eyes, and He sees His own dear Son's image there, and He takes him in. ~Charles H. Spurgeon, 1800s

Scripture

[T]o the praise of the glory of His grace, by which He has made us accepted in the Beloved. (Ephesians 1:6)

Bible Study

NO HUMAN SPIRIT THRIVES without a deep sense of acceptance. This represents a huge problem for a broken-down race, addicted to looking for love in all the wrong places. God designed the *family* as the fountainhead of acceptance and approval. Mom and Dad, when fulfilling their God-given design, fuel their children's gas tank with acceptance to last a lifetime.

That's the ideal.

Sadly, most of us run on fumes.

Whether it's young David, neglected by his father, or Moses, hidden in the bulrushes, or Jacob, desperately conniving a blessing from a father who thought him a wimp, the vacuum of parental disapproval sucks in whole constellations of dysfunction and pain.

If you've ever struggled with self-acceptance, there is beautiful hope for you. Your Heavenly Father reaches out to you with an acceptance that knows no bounds. He loves you as he loves Christ, and he approves of you to the same measure.

He not only loves you, he likes you. He enjoys you. He values your company.

The Bible says you are "accepted in the Beloved" (Ephesians 1:6). The Beloved is capitalized because it refers to the Beloved One, Jesus Christ.

In the Beloved One, by virtue of union with him, God accepts you just as much as he accepts Jesus. You are beloved in his sight, just like Jesus.

Any voices telling you the opposite are liars. Don't believe them. Don't listen to them. Don't curl up in a corner with Mr. Booze and indulge a pity party. By the Word of God and the Spirit of God, you can silence the accusing voices ever-ready to trash your worth.

When the prodigal son came home, the father ran to him and smothered him with kisses. Whether you've been prodigal much or not, that is God's response as often as you turn to him in faith.

You are beautiful in his eyes.

The Greek word translated "accepted" in Ephesians 1:6, sparkles with extra grace. One lexicon offers these definitions: "To make graceful, charming, lovely, agreeable. To pursue with grace, compass with favor. To honor with blessings."[6] I am blown away to think that

God pursues me with grace and compasses me with favor.

Disney has made a fortune telling stories of children desperately seeking their father's approval – think *Mary Poppins*, *The Sound of Music*, *Angels in the Outfield* (the remake), and *The Little Mermaid*.

May it comfort you to know, in good times and bad – whether you're on fire for God, or lukewarm before him, whether your behavior is decent or indecent – your truest Father approves of YOU, just as you are, in Christ. He delights in YOU. Even if your behavior is not so hot.

The next time you're tempted to berate yourself, reject yourself, or otherwise beat yourself up, let this beautiful reality crack through the crust of your self-rejection:

> The LORD your God in your midst, The Mighty One, will save; He will rejoice over you with gladness, He will quiet you with His love, He will rejoice over you with singing." (Zephaniah 3:17)

Additional Scriptures

Luke 15:23,24, Zephaniah 3:17, Isaiah 62:4.

Prayer

Dear Lord,

To think that you accept me as you accept Christ sometimes feels too good to be true. But it is true because you have said so. Today, I rest in this great reality. I bring my self-rejection to the foot of the Cross. I leave it there. I bring my performance anxieties, drives to achieve, obsessions over how I look, talk, act, and sound – Father, I lay them down at the Cross.

I lay my guilt and shame there too.

Lord, teach me to live with nothing left to prove.

I rest my soul in your perfect acceptance of me in Christ. I move into your embrace. I look for my worth to my Savior – he is all I need.

As often as the voices of accusation rise up in my head, O Lord, silence them with the voice of your Word.

As often as feelings of condemnation well up in my heart, O Lord, transform them by the power of your love.

When nobody accepts me, I know you accept me still. This is all the confidence I need to face my day.

Please create in me compassion for every fellow-pilgrim I encounter today.

By your grace, and for your glory,

Amen.

CHAPTER 12

I AM REDEEMED

Meditation

Jesus Christ has completely done the work of our redemption. He does not redeem us from some of our sins, and leave us to grapple with the rest. Oh, no! Christ makes a most complete work of it. He redeems us from all our iniquities. He delivers us out of the hands of all our enemies. He pays all debts, He delivers from all wrath, He takes off the whole curse, He saves to the uttermost, and will settle us in a state of full and perfect bliss – when grace shall be turned into glory. ~Thomas Brooks, 1675

Scripture

[K]nowing that you were not redeemed with corruptible things, like silver or gold, from your aimless conduct received by tradition from your fathers, but with the precious blood of Christ, as of a lamb without blemish and without spot. (1 Peter 1:18,19)

Bible Study

SHE WAS EMBARRASSED. Humiliated, really. Never in a million years did she think this would happen to her. She crossed boundaries she promised not to cross. She made choices she swore she would never make.

And now she wished with all her might she could erase them all from her memories. Wipe it all clean. Start over.

But she couldn't.

Never. And the worst part of it, right now, was the disgrace. Her secrets were no longer secrets. Her shame was paraded in front of everybody. Old friends. Neighbors. Everybody gave her "the look." They no longer made eye contact. They turned away. Mumbled hushed whispers to their partners. Took their kids by the hand and crossed the street.

And now... this... public humiliation. She stood atop a small marble block. Frozen. Naked. Fighting back tears.

A potential buyer eyed her head to toe. Circled her. His lingering gaze violated her soul. His hard breathing tied her stomach in knots.

The man chuckled and whispered an offer to her handler. The handler laughed. Shook his head. The buyer walked away disappointed.

The woman – the daughter of a man who disowned her – refused to let them see her cry.

She bore the ancient name, Gomer. Her husband was Israel's great spiritual leader, the prophet Hosea.

Gomer was a prostitute.

Hosea loved her. Married her. Cared for her. Entreated her to be faithful.

Gomer chased other lovers. She bore children by other men. She abandoned a faithful man and now would give anything to have him back.

But that was impossible. Her crooked path took her from the arms of one man to the next. Her needs dominated her. And meeting those needs... in secret trysts, in hurried actions, in acts of love without an ounce of love... meeting these needs was destroying her heart.

And she knew it.

She simply could not shake off the labels that drove her self-destruction.

Now, she stood on the auction block. Sold into slavery. A forgotten memory of Hosea's, she was sure.

Destined to be owned like a piece of meat. Ruled over. Another victim of the slave market of her own unbridled desire.

Who's Running Your Life?

Let me pause Gomer's story long enough to ask you a very big question. It's one of those questions a wise person will consider every once in a while.

Here is the question: Who's running your life?

Don't answer too quickly. Think about it. Most of us would quickly say, I'm running my life. Nobody tells me what to do.

Go deeper than that.

Could it be that your mountain of debt is running your life?

Could it be that the wounds of past abuse are running your life?

What about that next hit, that next drink, that next snack?

How about an obsession over your kids? Or your looks?

Or what about your perfectionism? The relentless compulsion to polish up that ironically painful label that says, "I'm perfect."

Some are killing themselves to be rich; the desire for money rules your life. Power. Sex. Porn. Lust. Money. Fame. Success. Status.

What obsession nags at you? or rules you? or owns you?

Think about it, because every time you make a choice that you kick yourself over a little while later, you are manifesting an area of emotional bondage.

And that emotional bondage means that your soul is marching to the beat of a little dictator from your past.

Slaves of Sin

Jesus said, "Most assuredly, I say to you, whoever commits sin is a slave of sin" (John 8:34). He was talking about unbelievers – no Christian can ever be a slave again – but the emotional structures can still remain long after you're saved.

This is emotional bondage. Every time you make a self-destructive choice, you prove exactly what the Bible has said for thousands of years: the human race has sold itself into the slave-market of sin. Our outward sins may be very different, but the shackled heart that beats within is no different than the one within that ancient woman, Gomer. A heart sold out to the highest bidder of the day.

Who can deliver us?

By his death on the Cross, Jesus shattered the prison bars of spiritual bondage through the power of REDEMPTION. God set me free through the shed blood of Christ.

Do you know that heaven has a theme song?

> And they sang a new song, saying: "You are worthy to take the scroll, / And to open its seals; / For You were slain, / And have redeemed us to God by Your blood / Out of every tribe and tongue and people and nation. (Revelation 5:9)

Hosea

I have to believe that Gomer heard the faintest echo of that song when she stood on that slave block long ago.

Deformed sexuality ruled her life. All she could do was to wait for the next master to buy her and use her. She waited, trembling, surrounded by filth, the smell of death, the weeping of slaves, the clanking of chains... the stench of despair.

But then she heard it. The faintest first whisper heaven's great song: "Worthy is the Lamb..." Only to her, it sounded like a familiar voice... a voice from her past.

"Gomer," he said.

She couldn't lift her eyes. She squeezed them shut against the intrusive gaze of other men's eyes.

But she heard her name again. "Gomer," the voice said. There was tenderness there.

A hand touched her chin. Lifted her face, gently. "Open your eyes," he said. Gomer opened her eyes to see the one person she never dreamt of seeing again.

There, in the slave market of sin was the man who loved her without limits. The man she cheated on, and ran away from.

There stood her own husband, Hosea – the prophet, the man of God – at the slave's auction block.

Hosea looked at the handler. "Name your price," he said.

And without flinching, Hosea paid that price in full. He bought his wife back to himself. This is what he wrote:

> Then the LORD said to me, "Go and get your wife again. Bring her back to you and love her, even though she loves adultery. For the LORD still loves Israel even though the people have turned to other gods, offering them choice gifts." So I bought her back for fifteen pieces of silver and about five bushels of barley and a measure of wine. (Hosea 3:1, 2, NLT)

Here's the amazing thing: He did not buy her as a *slave*; he bought her as a *person*. He paid the price not to own her, but to set her free.

This, in the Bible, is called redemption. Redemption means to buy a slave and set the slave free.

The Cross

You were in a slave market too.

You were a slave to sin, a slave to death, a slave to Satan, a slave to hell, and a slave to the flesh (your own fallen nature).

And Jesus set you free from all of it.

He didn't set you free by *power* only – busting into prison and flinging wide the doors. No, not by power only. He set you free by *payment*. That is what *redeem* means. It means to pay a price. It means to buy back. This wasn't an arm wrestling match, but a satisfaction of penalty and debt. Only then – *after* payment was complete – did Jesus deliver his epic haymaker to the devil's chin.

Redemption means to buy a slave and to set the slave free.

And what was the payment price? "The precious blood of Christ" (1 Peter 1:18, 19).

He didn't buy you to boss you around: he bought you to set you free. By shedding his blood, Christ satisfied every claimant against you. By joining you to Christ, God brought you into the monumental liberty of the children of God.

In your morality, your marriage, your finances, your sexuality, your dating – in your everything – you stand redeemed by the blood of Christ. By faith, walk into that freedom.

Whatever jail holds you, Jesus Christ has purchased you out of it. Nobody owns you but Jesus. Your sins don't own you. The devil doesn't own you. Your addictions don't own you. Your nasty reputation doesn't own you. Other people's labels don't own you. Your failures don't own you. The past doesn't own you. The people who hurt you don't own you. The Man, the government, shadowy conspirators, lousy genetics, disabilities, disease, cultish preachers don't own you.

You've been bought with a price, and it's time to be free. It's time to take hold of your blood-bought liberation day, and by faith, make spiritual redemption your everyday reality.

Additional Scriptures

Galatians 5:1, Revelation 5:9, 1 Corinthians 1:30; 6:20; 7:23.

Prayer

Precious Redeemer,
I declare today that no failure, no regret, no sin, no evil, no master, and no painful memory has the slightest authority over my life. You bought me back from those dark forces. You broke their chains and set me free. I belong to you.
I stand today redeemed by the blood of the Lamb. Jesus Christ delivered me from the slave market of sin. He shattered the bars of evil. He silenced the devil's roar. He broke the back of death and hell. Your Son, in one dark day on Calvary's Cross, set me free once for all from every malevolent force that would ever drag me down.
I take my stand today in the perfect liberty of Christ.
On his authority, and in his name, I tell the voices that would bind me, limit me, reduce me, and accuse me to be silent; they

have no authority in my life. Christ dethroned them, destroyed them, and demolished them.

I claim that truth by faith.

I declare it over myself and my family.

In Christ, I am free. My Redeemer is mighty. My redemption is complete.

Deliver me from limping beneath my dignity. Grant that I would walk worthy of my high calling. Teach me the grace to accept people as they are, without editing, fixing, constricting, or dominating them in any way; teach me to respect the freedom with which you have set them free.

In Christ's liberating grace,

Amen.

CHAPTER 13

I AM BLESSED

Meditation

It is a wonderful thing to be really one with a risen and exalted Savior, to be a member of Christ! Think what it involves. Can Christ be rich and I poor? ~Hudson Taylor, 1800s

Scripture

Blessed be the God and Father of our Lord Jesus Christ, who has blessed us with every spiritual blessing in the heavenly places in Christ. (Ephesians 1:3)

Bible Study

THERE IS NO SUCH THING as an unblessed Christian. If you are saved, you are blessed. Fully, richly, blessed. There's no stinginess with God's blessing. He drops down lavish boatloads of good stuff without measure and without price.

Most Christians make the soul-deadening mistake of coupling their daily performance with their level of blessing. To borrow a phrase, that's "stinkin' thinkin'." You are blessed because Christ is blessed, and you are in him. He is the blessed Son of God. In him, you share his blessings. His blessings are your blessings.

Let's make sure we're clear on what the word *blessing* actually means. A blessing is a gift of grace. It is the functional end of the grace pipeline. To bless is to give something good to someone without regard to merit or payment.

Earlier we affirmed that the single most important label in your life is the label you put on God.

Here's a label you need to peel off your God concept right now: *Employer.* God is not the heavenly boss, doling out paychecks for sweaty labor. God does not give paychecks; he gives blessings. He is not your employer; he is your Father. And he no more makes you work for your blessings than a loving father requires his toddlers to work for their Cheerios.

God gives blessings, not paychecks.

And therefore, you don't serve God for blessings.

If you had to work for them, they couldn't be called blessings, by definition.

Do you realize what this means?

Freely and Fully Blessed

This means God doesn't bless you because you studied your Bible this week. He doesn't bless you because you prayed extra hard, or because you went to church for a whole month of Sundays. You're not blessed more because you gave more – no matter what the prosperity preachers promise.

You are not blessed better because you cut out a nasty sin for a couple of weeks. And you are not blessed

114

less because of that episode of road rage you unleashed on that pokey old lady last week.

Quit working for blessings. Quit striving for blessings. Quit serving for blessings. Quit fasting, repenting, sweating, straining, and laboring for blessings.

The astounding fact of the gospel is God can't bless you any more than he has already blessed in you. You are blessed because Christ is blessed, and you are "in him."

Let that sink in.

On the day you were saved, in that golden moment you first believed, God dropped on your head an avalanche of blessings. He put your name on a stellar portfolio of assets for every need, and every circumstance, and every opportunity you will ever face for all the rest of eternity.

You are mind-blowingly blessed beyond your wildest dreams, and it happened in the very first nano-second of your salvation, of your union with Christ.

Says who?

Says God: you have been "blessed with EVERY spiritual blessing in the heavenly places in Christ Jesus" (Ephesians 1:3). That is a past tense, completed act, for every child of God.

Peter affirms, "...His divine power has given to us all things that pertain to life and godliness..." (2 Peter 1:3). Notice the verb: *has given*, in the past tense. So this is a done deal. Notice what was given: *all things* that pertain to life and godliness. Not a few things. Not fifty percent.

Not even nine-nine percent, and then go chase down that last one percent.

No.

All things.

Paul asks the question every triumphant spirit already knows the answer to:

> He who did not spare His own Son, but delivered Him up for us all, how shall He not with Him also freely give us all things? (Romans 8:32)

How shall He not?

Answer: it's impossible to even conceive of it. To even imagine that the same generous God who was willing to give the astonishing gift of a beloved Son would suddenly grow stingy over a loaf of bread. How shall he not?

All things. There's your blessing.

If he gave you the hardest gift of all when he gave you Jesus, won't he with much more ease give you all the lesser gifts of life's relatively little blessings?

Let this promise flood your mind and heart: "And my God shall supply all your need according to His riches in glory by Christ Jesus" (Philippians 4:19).

You can't not be blessed, because you are in Christ, and he is eternally blessed.

Feeling Blessed

But you object: when the zombie apocalypse looms just over the horizon, and Dr. Jellyfinger offers nothing but bad news, how can you say I'm blessed? That's just crazy!

Let us now contemplate the difference between *being* blessed, which you are, and *feeling* blessed, which you might or might not be.

Just because you *are* blessed, it doesn't mean you *feel* blessed. Just because you are rich, it doesn't mean you feel rich. Just because you are loved, it doesn't mean you feel loved. Just because... well, point made.

The day after you're saved, you're still the same person you were the day before you were saved, but with one very huge difference: you are a new creation, identity-wise. Your new identity now orbits your union with Christ; you are no longer sold to sin as a slave to your flesh (your fallen, corrupted, guilty nature).

Your flesh has been dethroned, declawed, defanged, and defeated. You are not "in the flesh," and you can never be again. The Holy Spirit lives in you. Christ lives in you. And where Christ dwells, evil cannot occupy.

But you probably don't feel that way. You still have memories of your pre-saved days. You still have habits. Maybe there's a long list of lies you believe. Maybe your whole worldview has been pieced together by an army of little gollums, or brats, or thugs, or spoiled little princesses, or judgmental, legalistic, self-righteous Pharisees.

Past programming haunts you as you head into your new life in Christ. That's the source of your defeated spirit, your perpetual victim-status, your addiction, your hardness, and the mother of all your dysfunctions. And even if you were saved in childhood, you still swim every day in a sea of spiritual monsters. There's no way to live in this world without contracting the grime of depravity.

Even so...

You are a new CREATION.

But you are still living with old IDEATION.

So what do you need most?

You need TRANSFORMATION, BY THE RENEWING OF YOUR MIND, which is the whole purpose of your *Grace Rehab.*

That's the only way your *feelings* will ever catch up to the *truth* God says about you in Christ.

There's a beautiful prayer in the Old Testament, offered by a royally messed up King David, after the most heinous sin of his erratic life: "restore unto me the joy of your salvation" (Psalm 51:12). He doesn't pray for a restored salvation, because salvation is impossible to lose.

He prays for restored joy. He prays, not for blessing, but for the feeling of being blessed.

You might accuse me of picking at straws. It's a distinction without a difference, you might say.

But actually, it's all the difference in the world.

The gospel of God does not send you forth on a lifelong errand to earn your blessings.

It sends you forth to believe in the blessings that became yours once for all in the hour you first believed.

Write this down, make a poster, set it as your laptop's wallpaper, tattoo it across your soul, if not your forearm: *You don't serve God for blessing; you serve God from blessing.*

Look around yourself every day. Really notice *people* – the celebrities whose faces gawk at you from the tabloids, the sports legends, and your everyday friends at work, school, and in the hood. Notice them, and let this truth wrap around your soul: *you are the richest person you see.* You are blessed to the maximum. God can't bless you any more than he already has blessed you.

If you could fly up to heaven right now, you'd see a huge pile of beautifully wrapped gifts with your name on them. These gifts are your blessings. Long before you were born, God looked down the corridors of time. He previewed your life. He saw every need, every circumstance, every trial, and every opportunity you would face. He knew your joys before you lived them. Your sorrows, too. God knew.

But he did more than just know.

God also provided. The Great Yahweh Yireh, the Lord Who Provides, pre-prepared absolutely perfect provision for every moment of your life yet to come. Whatever supply you need, it's there. Whatever health, whatever wealth, whatever ideas, whatever courage, whatever *whatever* you need has been pre-supplied, pre-packaged, and pre-arranged. This doesn't mean you'll always be healthy or wealthy, but it does mean you'll be rich in treasures money can't buy.

And one thing you should know about God: he is never late. Yes, he seems slow. Is that because he's so old? No. It's because his ways are higher than our ways, and his timing is perfect.

Paul said, "All things are yours" (1 Corinthians 3:21).

The old hymn-writer sang, "Every need, His hand supplieth."

May your heart say, "Amen!"

Don't Fall For the Devil's Lies

The devil works overtime to convince you of a lie. He wants you to doubt God's blessings. Maybe God won't provide for you. Maybe he doesn't care. Maybe God isn't strong enough. Or maybe you're just too unworthy. After all, look at the mess you've made! God may bless other people, but not you.

So you think.

And so you would be wrong. That warped faith in the anti-christ is the kiss of death to your salvation's joy. You've turned grace on its head. You've made the classic mistake of confusing a blessing with a paycheck. You need rehab.

Study the Scriptures. Pore over the divine testament, the Bible. You will find this counter-intuitive reality: God never has, and never will, bless you because you've made yourself worthy. He blesses you because you've been joined to the Worthy One, the Lord Jesus Christ, by faith. So discover your possessions in Christ. Count your blessings; name them one by one if you have to. Lay hold of your riches in Christ.

Tune your heart to sing his praise, and one day you'll wake up smack dab in the middle of a God-blessed life that actually *feels* blessed.

There's a great story about pioneer missionary Hudson Taylor packing up his family to go to the unreached masses of mainland China. In an age before telephones and Internet, his friends warned him, "You will be forgotten in that dark land."

Taylor replied, "I have two children. I have no problem remembering when they must eat. I know when they are tired. I know when they need a pillow for their heads. I do not forget my children. If I, a poor earthly father, can never forget my children or their needs, neither will my Heavenly Father forget me. No, I will not be forgotten."

That is the testimony of a person who can say every single day, come hell or high water, "I am blessed."

Additional Scriptures

Philippians 4:19, Micah 7:7, Psalm 23, 2 Corinthians 9:8.

Prayer

Gracious Father,

I acknowledge today you have blessed me better than I deserved. Not only that, you have blessed me to the full. You have granted every spiritual blessing, and all things that pertain to life and godliness. All things are mine in Christ.

I am blessed because I am in Christ.

You know, Lord, the many times I have tried to buy a blessing from you. But today I won't do that, because your blessings aren't for sale. They are the blood-bought gifts of my Savior's perfect grace. I could never afford them, not in a million years of works and a million acts of contrition.

So I am blessed because Christ is blessed and I am one with him.

Thank you for such magnificent blessings. Thank you for a supernatural portfolio of everyday assets. Thank you for knowing my need and meeting it too. You are perfect in this. You have never let me down. I bless the God who has blessed my life.

I ask you, Lord, to restore to me the joy of my salvation. Grow in me the faith to feel my blessings, to see them with my own eyes, and to rest in your perfect provision and love.

I reject a whiny spirit. I reject a heart of victimization and despair. I will not live out of a sense of deficit today.

Instead, I will rest my soul in your overflowing love.

In this world so full of darkness, let me shine the light of a God-blessed life. Let others see your good hand upon me. And may they then turn, that they may find in you, the treasure that I have found because I found the Lord.

In Christ's Matchless Grace,
Amen.

CHAPTER 14

I HAVE AN ADVOCATE

Meditation

But in seasons of darkness and distress, when guilt from repeated backslidings lies hard and heavy on the conscience; when the mists and fogs of unbelief gather over the foundations of our hope; when our evidences are beclouded and our signs but dimly seen, then we need a living Advocate who can plead our cause, we being unable to do it ourselves, and by presenting on our behalf his blood and obedience, his sufferings, sacrifice, and death, may bring us off more than conquerors against every accusing plea and every opposing adversary. ~J. C. Philpot, 1800s

Scripture

My little children, these things I write to you, so that you may not sin. And if anyone sins, we have an Advocate with the Father, Jesus Christ the righteous. (1 John 2:1)

Bible Study

WHEN I WAS A KID, CHRISTMAS lights weren't these dinky little things we have today; they were bulky strands of light bulbs, each bigger than a fat grape. If you stepped on them, they popped.

I think that's the motive the strange man from down the street suspected when he discovered that neighborhood vandals had crushed his strand of outdoor Christmas lights. He knocked at our door. My dad answered. I stood several steps behind him, on the light-brown shag carpet in the living room. The man accused me of breaking his Christmas lights.

My dad looked across the room at me, and asked if I'd broken this man's Christmas lights.

I denied everything.

"Well, Sir," my dad said, "if my son says he didn't do it, he didn't do it. I have to stick up for my son."

The man had his doubts, I'm sure, but what else could he do? He walked away.

I breathed a sigh of relief.

My dad went to bat for me that day. Whether or not I'd actually done the deed doesn't matter at this point. Right? My dad was on my side. He protected me. He stood between his son and the accuser, and sent the accuser packing.

Thank God for my advocate.

Parakletos

The Greek word, *parakletos*, is rich in meaning. Depending on context, it can mean helper, comforter, strengthener, fortifier, assistant, or defense attorney.

When John called Christ our Advocate, he did so in the context of a legal case against our sins. "If anyone sins," if anyone stands under accusation, he says, if anyone is caught in the act – not potentially, but actually – then what? That is the setup.

In the Supreme Court of heaven, an innocent person needs no defense. But that's exactly the point. There are no innocent persons. So we all need a good lawyer.

Aren't you thankful for your Advocate, Jesus Christ?

He's got your back. He'll stick up for you. He's on your side. The whole world might abandon you, but Jesus never will.

The beautiful thing about your heavenly Advocate is that he never argues fiction. He never spins the truth. He never shades what actually happened in order to get you off.

Instead, he faces the truth squarely and honestly. He points out to the judge, that though you crushed the Christmas lights, the penalty has already been paid. He shows his wounded hands and names you as his own. He reminds a Judge who needs no reminding that the scales of justice are balanced forever by the precious blood of Christ.

Your sins: PAID IN FULL.

Your embarrassing secrets: PAID IN FULL.

Your errors and omissions: PAID IN FULL.

Your crimes: PAID IN FULL.

Your bratty behavior and tantrums: PAID IN FULL.

Your lukewarmness toward Jesus: PAID IN FULL.

Your bullying: PAID IN FULL.

Your darkest shame: PAID IN FULL.

Jesus, your Advocate, stands forever as heaven's proof that all the murky boatload of evil, sin, dysfunction and despair that you bring to the table has been washed clean, completely, in full, once for all and forever, by Calvary's love.

Not in theory, but in reality.

And time after time, the truth remains: the court has no choice but to rule in your favor.

The devil shouts, "You're guilty! I saw you! You're guilty!"

Jesus gives him "the look" and he scurries away with his forked tail between his slithery legs.

That is the power of the cross.

Please don't buy into the mistaken impression that the Father is stern and angry, so the Son has to soften him up. No. Every Person in the Godhead loves you with an equal love, and is utterly committed to your well-being. Christ wouldn't be your Advocate if the Father didn't send him and the Spirit didn't empower him.

Don't sin, says St. John. I'm writing so that you don't sin.

But if you do, don't freak out. Don't give up. Don't quit on God. Don't punish yourself. Don't wallow in guilt and shame.

You are not alone. Someone is on your side, and he makes all the difference.

You have an Advocate with the Father.

Jesus Christ, the righteous.

And that is one lawyer that can never lose.

Additional Scriptures

Hebrews 9:24, 7:25, 1 John 2:2.

Prayer

Precious Lord,

Thank you for my invincible Advocate, your Son, Jesus. Who better to stand in my place? What better representative before your heavenly courts could a human ever desire?

You say you've cast down the "Accuser" of God's people – the devil – and you have (Revelation 12:10). He'll never win a case against Jesus.

Though my sins should buffet me, though my guilt should crush the spirit out of me, though my failures and crimes weigh heavily on my mind, I turn to my Advocate, and find peace.

I confess, O God, I did the crime.

But I confess by faith, O Judge of the Living and Dead, Christ did the time.

So when my Advocate argues for my release, he has an airtight case. Heaven lays no charge against me. The devil has no power against me. My sins, however heinous, neither define me nor confine me.

I am ruled not guilty and I am declared righteous once for all through the perfect Advocacy of Jesus Christ. I rest my heart today in the One who loved me, and never ceases to rise in my defense.

Help me, Gracious Father, to sound forth Christ's advocacy for my friends today who struggle with guilt and shame.

In the name of my Advocate, I pray,

Amen.

CHAPTER 15

I HAVE ACCESS

Meditation

Do not live as if God were as far off from you as the east is from the west. Live not far below on the earth; but live on high, as if you were in heaven. In heaven you will be with God; but on earth He will be with you: is there much difference? ~Charles H. Spurgeon, 1800s

Scripture

Through whom also we have access by faith into this grace in which we stand, and rejoice in hope of the glory of God. (Romans 5:2)

Therefore, brethren, having boldness to enter the Holiest by the blood of Jesus, by a new and living way which He consecrated for us, through the veil, that is, His flesh, and having a High Priest over the house of God, let us draw near with a true heart in full assurance of faith, having our hearts sprinkled from an evil conscience and our bodies washed with pure water. (Hebrews 10:19-22)

Bible Study

M Y DAD, ROY – NOW IN HEAVEN – grew up in Chicago loving baseball, especially the Chicago Cubs. As a kid, he routinely rode the bus to Wrigley Field where he could breathe the air the "friendly confines." Once there, he'd join the pack of kids waiting on Waveland Avenue, behind left field. If a batter was strong enough, he could slam an out-of-the-park home run; it would land on Waveland with a huge bounce, and all the kids would scramble for the prize.

The biggest prize, however, was to score a ticket and get inside.

One lazy Sunday afternoon, young Roy had a thought. He eyed the walls separating himself from his beloved Cubs. The smell of popcorn and peanuts, the roar of the crowd inside, and the thought of ivy-covered walls were too much. He couldn't take being an outsider any more. So he did what any youthful, red-blooded baseball fan of that era would do: he started climbing the left-field wall. He scoped out a climbing path, and started climbing.

He made it about twelve feet above ground before he got busted

A man in a suit called to him, my dad said, and made him climb down. Then that man told young Roy to come with him. Roy was scared. His mind ran scenarios of how his strict Italian parents would react. Roy thought of running, but the man had ushers with him. He thought of pleading, but the man looked too stern.

He walked along in silence, looking for any way out of his doom. His palms sweated. His heart pounded. The man walked my dad to the nearest entrance to Wrigley Field. He walked him through the gates, through the turnstiles, past the gatekeepers. Past security. His mind raced. Would they call the cops? On the way in, Roy heard the most magical words he could imagine: "Good afternoon, Mr. Wrigley."

That man in that suit – that man who called my dad down from his climbing and escorted him to his personal front row seats to enjoy the game – that man was Philip K. Wrigley, son of William Wrigley, whose gum you've probably chewed, and whose hapless baseball team you've probably scorned.

The son brought my dad past the barrier and gave him access to his heart's deepest desires.

Access

God's Son did the same for you.

That mountain of sin that barred you from God: removed.

That burden of debt that crushed your hopes: paid in full.

That wall of divine holiness, that fire of divine presence, that fear of infinite company: breached, quenched, resolved.

Whatever barrier stood between you and Heaven's Mighty God has been demolished and removed once and for all.

Through Christ's Cross, and now by virtue of union with him, you have an all-access pass to the heavenly realms. It's valid right now. Here on earth. Even before you die and go to heaven. You have access.

You can approach God anyplace, any time, for any reason. When you pray, you can be confident he is as near as your prayer's first breath.

You can approach him boldly. No groveling needed. God's children don't beg. They rise to their full stature before heaven's throne, state their needs, thank their Father, and get on with their day. Do not fear to approach your King. He is mighty to save, and loves your biggest requests.

I have this suspicion that when we finally see the Savior face to face, he won't berate us for bringing him prayers that were too big.

When you approach, approach him boldly, without fear. Come into his presence without the slightest doubt of his willing acceptance. He wants your company. He enjoys your conversation. He seeks you that you might seek him.

You can approach him immediately. You do not need to prep. You do not need to primp. No preliminaries needed. No reduction of sin. No improvement of your Ten Commandments batting average. No contrition over wrongs you have done. He says to come and to come boldly. So do it without hesitation. Come just as you are.

You can approach him directly. Do not attempt to reach him through intermediaries. You need no saint, no priest, no pastor, and no pope – not even Mary – to soften up God before you arrive.

You have an all-purpose Mediator in Christ, and he is the only one you need (1 Timothy 2:5).

How would you like it if your child always sent a few envoys ahead of lunch to find out your mood and to ask for extra fries? You'd know something was wrong in the relationship.

And so it is with God. You have 24/7 access to the King of kings and Lord of lords. He knows you personally. And he likes you.

Peel off any labels that make you feel like an unwelcome outsider. God labels you part of his innermost circle.

Believe it.

The heavenly security team is waiting for you – they've been briefed. They know your name. They won't stop you. The heavenly gates are opened for you. Walk through with a full assurance of faith. The heavenly table is set for you. Come and dine on the richest of fare. Access is yours. No barriers in sight.

Right now, Almighty God waits for you with eager anticipation.

What are you waiting for?

Additional Scriptures

Romans 5:2, Ephesians 2:18; 3;12, Hebrews 4:16.

Prayer

Gracious Father,

How I bless you for this tremendous access to the courts of heaven. The throne of grace is there for me, for your Son has opened the way. No angel will stop me and no demon can try. Not even the devil can bar me from you.

Yet sometimes, I hesitate. I think you're mad at me, or I delude myself into needless preliminaries. I'm sorry for that. But I profess today: my sins don't exclude me, my guilt can't blockade me, and nothing I can ever do or fail to do will shut me out from your holy presence.

So, Father, I draw near in full assurance of faith.

I come to you in my need. I come to you in my sorrows. I come to you in my joys. I come to you for everything and for nothing.

In your presence, I find peace in my problems, clarity in my perplexity, and comfort in the dark night of my soul. I find the embrace of a Father, the familiarity of a friend, and safety of an advocate and protector.

I find rest for my soul.

All those things that worry me, I lay at your feet. I let them go. In your time, do your mighty work. I have access to heaven; what on earth can steal my joy?

Let me never forget what it felt like to be an outsider with you, back before I met Jesus. And grant me a deep compassion for those who still must be brought into the fold.

In Christ I pray,

Amen

CHAPTER 16

I AM COMPLETE IN HIM

Meditation

In every position of danger or duty Christ Himself is all-sufficient for protection or support. Under every conceivable or inconceivable trial, we shall find in Him sufficient grace: should every earthly stream be dried, there is enough in Him, in the absence of them all. His glorious person is the dwelling-place of all-sufficiency. "In Him dwelleth all the fulness of the Godhead bodily;" as the fulness of Deity is sufficient to create and sustain a universe of ponderous orbs, and whole worlds of living creatures, can it be supposed that it will be found unable to supply the necessities of saints? ~Charles H. Spurgeon, 1800s

Scripture

For in Him dwells all the fullness of the Godhead bodily; and you are complete in Him, who is the head of all principality and power. (Colossians 2:9,10)

Bible Study

CHRIST IS NO HALF-SAVIOR, he never grants a partial salvation, and there's no such thing as an incomplete Christian. As he possesses the fullness of the divine nature, so he bestows the fullness of complete salvation.

You are in him.

He is complete.

You are complete in him.

Your *legal union* is complete, and you can obtain no better status, and no greater blessings than what you have already attained. Perfect is perfect and you are perfect in God's sight.

No matter what your in-laws say.

Your *mystical union* is complete, and there is no more of Christ to move into you. All of Christ occupies you, meshes with you, and empowers you, day by day, to think like Jesus and to live like Jesus. When Jesus took up residence within you, he didn't come in parts. And he didn't come with an off switch. All that he has to bring, he has already brought. All that he plans to do, he's already doing. Christ lives in you fully, totally, and to the max.

Quit asking for more of Jesus or of his Spirit.

Your *moral union*, however, is incomplete; you still have some growing to do. You still have Christlikeness to develop. You still have faith to feed. The completeness Jesus brought into you has not been completely experienced by you.

However, the distinction is super-important: just as you don't serve God for blessing, but from blessing, so you don't serve him for completeness, but from completeness. And you set your sights on rising up emotionally and experientially to your truest self in Christ.

To walk through life feeling you have missing parts is to doom yourself to a second rate Christianity.

You're the real deal, with the fullest possible package of blessing and dignity and grace. Your struggle is not to *get*, for you can't get any more of Jesus or from Jesus than you already have. Your struggle is not to *get*, but to *believe* what you have gotten.

That's why you're reading this book, I hope.

What Won't Complete You

Getting revenge on perpetrators from your past won't complete you. Neither will a remorseful apology from them. You've got to let go. Yes, call the authorities and stop further crimes – or legally deal with past crimes – where possible, but realize your wholeness and well-being do not depend on what perpetrators do or don't do, face or don't face. God will handle them: he promised to (Hebrews 10:30).

Finding a pot of gold coins while walking your dog won't complete you (this actually happened, worth $10 million[7]). Neither will winning the lottery, being left a big inheritance, or landing the dream job at the dream salary.

You are complete without those things. Before you ever got those things. And if you don't believe that, then achieving those things will only, in the long run, birth more frustrations than they solve.

This should not cause laziness in you or passivity: "Yawn, I'm complete in Christ, so I'll play another ten hours of video games." No. It should motivate courage to craft a life of risk, adventure, and bold love: "Hooray, I'm complete in Christ! Now, it's time to figure out a cure for cancer!"

You may be single, and wish you were married. You may be married, and wish you were single. You may yearn for children. You may yearn for the day your children leave home. You may ache over years of unanswered prayers, believing the day of your miracle will be the day of your completion.

Yet God has said:

> "My grace is sufficient for you, for My strength is made perfect in weakness." Therefore most gladly I will rather boast in my infirmities, that the power of Christ may rest upon me. (2 Corinthians 12:9)

Translation: You are complete in Christ long before you are complete in the answers to your prayer.

You need not look for completeness to sources outside your life. You do not look to your husband or wife. Or to your ex. Or to your next husband or wife. You do not look to your children. Or grandchildren. Or adoptive children.

Don't look to your ministry, or your preaching, or your shelves full of published books. Your batting average, or the trophies on your shelf. Your muscular selfies, or the applause of adoring fans.

While these blessings can be legitimate sources of satisfaction and joy, without a deep-rooted acceptance of God's acceptance of you in Christ, your soul will never find rest. You will always feel incomplete, no matter how may awards you stack on top of your pile of gold.

You'll always need another accolade, another contract, another child, another success.

Unfair Expectations

If you're waiting for that moment when the unlikely hero bursts into the room full of commiserating friends and tearfully announces, "You complete me," to be happy, you're going to have a frustrating life. And you're going to be a pain to be around.

That expectation is unfair. You're setting up other people for failure. Nobody else can make you happy. Nobody else can complete you.

Just Jesus.

And he has completed you, the day you were saved. In that glorious moment you received complete forgiveness from a complete salvation, offering complete care for all your days. God's power is complete for you, his love is complete toward you, and his presence is complete in you. You have complete resources for every need of every day. You have complete competency for every crisis. You have complete sufficiency for every circumstance.

You are not a puzzle box with missing pieces. You are not damaged goods. You didn't stand in the wrong line when God was passing out blessings.

That unfinished book on your laptop, that unfolded laundry in your kitchen, that unresolved issue with your drug-addled brother... God isn't like that at all. Whatever he starts, he finishes. Whatever he launches, he pushes through to stick a perfect landing.

You can do all things in Christ because you are all things in Christ. You are complete in him.

Believe it. Walk in it by faith. And live a life of bold adventure, knowing it's not success that completes you, but Christ alone.

Additional Scriptures

2 Peter 1:3, 2 Corinthians 3:5; 9:8, 1 Corinthians 1:30,31.

Prayer

Dear God,
I take my stand on this truth today: I am complete in Christ.
No matter what I face, I have complete sufficiency in him. No matter what I need, I have complete provision in him. No matter what I do, I have complete power in him.
When I feel inadequate, you are the all-sufficient one.
When I feel afraid, you are the God of all mercies.
When I hurt, you are the Father of all comforts.
When I face today's challenges, you are Lord over them all.
So many times, Lord, I feel defeated. My deficits own my thinking. My deficiencies rule my days. I label myself BROKEN. INCOMPLETE. Yet you've declared me complete in Christ, and on that reality I take my stand.
Nothing is lacking. No blessing is missing. No need is omitted in your perfect design of me. The person I was before I met Christ is not who I am today. Christ is in me, and I am in him forever. I am a new creation, made perfect and whole. Lord, even my imperfections are only windows for your grace to shine more brightly through me.
I will not wait for other people to complete me – with or without their apologies or approval, I am whole and complete in You. I will not wait for an answered prayer to complete me – I already have all I need in You.

By faith, I rise up to my full stature in Christ.

By faith, I refuse to slink beneath my identity or slouch beneath my dignity.

By faith, I refute the devil's lies that I am damaged goods or beyond repair.

By faith I can do all things in Christ because I have all things in Christ and I am all things in Christ. He is my treasure, my fortress, my shield, my success, and my all in all.

That is my hope today, dear Lord. That is my declared intention. Grow and increase this faith in me, I pray,

Through Christ,

Amen.

CHAPTER 17

I HAVE POWER

Meditation

Many Christians estimate difficulty in the light of their own resources, and thus they attempt very little and they always fail. All giants have been weak men who did great things for God because they reckoned on His power and presence to be with them. ~Hudson Taylor, 1800s

Scripture

I can do all things through Christ who strengthens me. (Philippians 4:13)

Bible Study

SUPERNATURAL, DIVINE POWER is the birthright of every child of God. In the Bible, St. Paul prayed for you to personally experience the power of God. Specifically, he prayed you would experience the same power that raised Christ from the dead (Ephesians 1:19). It's hard to doubt God's empowering presence when you read verses like this:

> Now to Him who is able to do exceedingly abundantly above all that we ask or think, according to the power that works in us, to Him be glory in the church by Christ Jesus to all generations, forever and ever. Amen. (Ephesians 3:20, 21)

To me, that weirdly combines both good news and bad news. The good news is that God stands ready to flex his massive biceps to work in, for, and through my life.

The bad news is that I so rarely feel that power. When it comes to supernatural expressions of divine power, I must have been standing in the wrong line most of my life. I've never dropped a giant with a sling and a stone, never healed the sick, and never parted a sea. Whereas the power of God caused Peter to walk on water, I'm nothing but a sinker. I've never made a mountain move. Never caused a wall to crumble. And never caused the blind to see, the deaf to hear, or the sick to be made immediately well.

At a pastor's conference, I had a long discussion with a fellow pastor. He had struggled with even becoming a Christian, he said, because of this issue of power: "The Bible talks about all these miracles, and then I looked at Christians and said, 'Where's the power?'"

I look at myself most days and ask the same question.

If God's mighty muscles operate in and through my life, I must be doing something wrong. Why can't I respond better when my [super-adorable, fantastic] kids drive me nuts? Why can't I lose the unwanted weight? Why can't I be more consistent with Scripture and prayer? If I am the living conduit for the dazzling power of God, why am I such a fizz?

Where's my miracle?

Where's the power?

I've struggled long and hard with these questions, and I don't think I'm alone. My hunch is you're with me – at least a little – or you wouldn't have picked up a book with this title.

What can we say about God's power in a Christian's life?

Power Lesson One

The first lesson of the power of God is the most counter-intuitive: *there is no official feeling of the power of God.*

God doesn't always announce his power with angelic choirs or flashes. He whispers his power in the "still small voice" (I Kings 19:12, KJV). He magnifies his power in your frailty and weakness (2 Corinthians 12:9). He reveals his power in the message of the death-dealing Cross (1 Corinthians 1:18).

It's taken me a long time to realize I've been looking for God's power in all the wrong places. I was looking for drama, for razzle-dazzle, for immediate answers to prayer.

And God is certainly able, and more willing than we think, to do a miracle and flash his glory across the sky.

But his usual mode inverts those polarities.

God's power shines in the tear-streaked face of a weeping mother, upholding her addicted son in prayer.

His power enables the grief-stricken widow to shower a grandson with kindness.

When sleep-deprived parents of a fussy toddler push through another night, and can manage a smile and a hug, the angels of heaven cheer.

When a player on the losing team pats the winner on the back, when a half-broke single mom returns the excess change to the grocery clerk, when a person who's received no good answers to prayer bows the knee again anyway, the power of God flashes across the cosmos as a spectacle to dazzle the demons.

What exactly does the power of God feel like?

Weakness or strength.

Sadness or joy.

Cowardice or confidence.

Heartache or heartburn.

The power of God feels like whatever feeling you feel right now as you read these words. The power of God can flow through you and work for you in any situation, with any feeling, any emotion, any physical state, and any digestive status at all.

"...when I am weak, then I am strong" (2 Corinthians 12:10).

Why? Because there is no official feeling of the power of God.

Quit labeling yourself weak. Reject the labels of wimp, coward, pushover, and doormat. Sometimes, it's a bigger miracle that you walk with dignity through a storm than that the winds stop blowing.

I would like to free you from the endlessly frustrating chase for more power, more zing, or more sizzle from

God. You have something far better, and it's always in your reach.

You have the indwelling power of Christ flowing through you, 24/7.

How does that work?

Power Lesson Two

The second lesson of the power of God is simple: the power of God flows for you whenever faith flows in you.

Faith unleashes the power of God. It's like a light switch: to turn on the faith is to turn on the power. God's power goes to work in "us who believe" (Ephesians 1:19).

As often as you believe, the power of God is unleashed. Faith turns on the power.

But you say, I tried faith, and it didn't work. Maybe the bulb was unplugged.

No.

If you tried faith, it did work. Faith always accomplishes what God wants to be accomplished. Without fail. Faith in God's Word can't fail. And a person of faith can't be a failure. When you show your faith, God shows his power. Even if you don't feel it. Even if you don't see it (remember Power Lesson One above).

His power can feel like comfort. His power can feel like being held in his hands, upheld by everlasting arms (Deuteronomy 33:27). His power can feel like peace in a storm, or like clarity in a fight. By his power you can smile through tears, press through fears, and keep faith with God through years of disappointment or loss. His power can also feel like supernatural strength, wisdom, and courage from on high – like you can put to flight armies of enemies.

The point is the faith, not how the power feels.

Because your faith wins the applause of heaven. Your faith is precious to God – especially faith in times when faith makes no sense.

Even better, your faith stockpiles massive treasures in heaven for your eternal fun.

Best of all, your faith accomplishes the will of God in your place at your time, even if it seems as if everything you trusted God for happened backwards.

Power Lesson Three

That's because of the third lesson of God's power: *your job is faith; God's job is outcomes.*

Most Christians confuse positive outcomes with divine power. We say, "Wow, the power of God was really at work because my aching bunion just got healed." True enough. But God's power would be equally displayed if the bunion didn't get healed, and you moved forward in life with thankfulness, dignity, and grace, despite the awkward gait.

The outcomes are not in your control; they are secondary. They are not your responsibility. Your job is faith; God's job is outcomes. And those outcomes are brilliantly designed by God to, a) bless you (experientially) in ways you didn't see coming, and, b) further God's mighty redemptive purposes in the world in ways nobody saw coming.

Which is harder: trusting God when the prayer is immediately answered, or trusting God when the heavens seem like a brick wall, and your prayer ricochets to smack you in the face?

The person who walks in faith after unanswered prayer is a living, breathing, four-dimensional testament of the mighty power of God.

In case it isn't clear, I'm bending over backwards to get you to quit looking at your world the way the world looks at the world. God does not see as humans see. We look at the outward appearance. But God is looking at the heart.

Yes, never stop praying for your miracle. Until it comes, quit looking for power in all the wrong places.

Start looking for faith, and the power will flow. You have power. All you need. You have an infinity of it.

But your power looks funny. It's a "treasure in jars of clay" (2 Corinthians 4:7, NIV). It's sometimes wrapped "in weakness, in fear, and in much trembling" (1 Corinthians 2:3). It looks like foolishness and smells like weakness (1 Corinthians 1:27). Yet it is the omnipotence of God omnisciently manifested through a Christian's daily routine.

Do you need power?

It's already waiting for you. Walk in faith and go move that mountain. One speck at a time.

Additional Scriptures

Zechariah 4:6, 2 Corinthians 3:5, Ephesians 1:15-23, 1 Kings 19:9-12.

Prayer

Father,

I stand before you today an heir of the mighty power of my Lord Jesus Christ. He is strong in me. He is strong in good times and bad, in triumph and defeat, in sickness and health.

I claim his power as my own. Power to love. To serve. To handle the storms of life. To forgive. To work. To play. To change yet another diaper. To dig yet another ditch. To endure yet another day of difficulty and pain.

In Christ, I have all the power I need.

Your grace, O Lord, is sufficient for me. Your power is enough and more than enough.

I admit that sometimes I doubt your power. I don't feel it, so I don't believe it. Sorry. Sometimes, I'm enamored of the fireworks display. Teach me to trust you without it, dear God.

Help me to see your power today in the humblest works of your hand. When I feel weak, help me lean on your magnificent strength.

I know you can do miracles, God. Your hand is "not shortened" that it cannot save. So I ask for the miracle. I pray for the victory. I seek you for the best outcome of all.

Until that day comes, whether in this life or the next...

I will not let the voices of defeat define me. I will not let the emotion of despair wreck me. I will walk in dignity. I will stand in faith. Though a thousand foes gather against, me, I will stand, firmly rooted, in a God will "do exceedingly, abundantly above all" that I could ask or think (Ephesians 3:20).

In the things that scare me, I claim Christ's courage.

In the things that overwhelm me, I claim Christ's power.

In the things that intimidate me, I claim Christ's triumph.

In all things that come against me today, I claim Christ's Spirit, and walk in his almighty power.

I say with faith, I can do all things this day through Christ who gives me strength.

And today, I pray, that you will orchestrate the details of my life, so that somebody I know would embrace my mighty Savior because of my daily life's testimony of his great strength.
In Jesus' Mighty Name,
Amen.

CHAPTER 18

I HAVE DOMINION

Meditation

God means every Christian to be effective, to make a difference in the actual records and results of Christian work. God put each of us here to be a power. There is not one of us but is an essential wheel of the machinery and can accomplish all that God calls us to. ~A.B. Simpson, 1800s

Scripture

For if, by the trespass of the one man, death reigned through that one man, how much more will those who receive God's abundant provision of grace and of the gift of righteousness reign in life through the one man, Jesus Christ. (Romans 5:17, NIV)

Bible Study

AT CREATION, GOD GAVE Adam and Eve dominion over their lives and their world (Genesis 1:26-28). They possessed the sparkling scepter of planet earth, a gracious bestowal of God.

At the Fall – when Adam sinned – he dropped that scepter, surrendering his dominion to a Pandora's box of nasty tyrants. The human story tells the sad tale of a mad scramble to claim the scepter.

Who rules your life?

Who rules your world?

Don't be too quick to answer. Think about it.

Many might say, "I rule my life." I rule my world. If you are godly Christian person, you might say, "God rules my life. I told Jesus to take the wheel, and he has."

That's great.

But let's go deep.

Who's really running your life? In a brutally honest moment, some might say, My debt runs my life. Every day, I spend all kinds of emotion wringing my hands over the hole I've dug. I'm working overtime to pay off my stupid debt. Most conversations with my spouse end in a fight over money. Debt wields the scepter in my life, and beats me on the head with it day by day.

Somebody else might say, My crazy father runs my life. His addictions define me. His labels own me. My deepest emotions swirl down the toilet of his cruelty, his absence, his abuse, his unavailability. I exhaust myself managing the needless drama of my dysfunctional family tree. The crazy memories of my past run my life.

Yet another might confess, My addictions run my life. All I think about is the next hit, the next drink, the next roll of the dice, the next click of the mouse and the images it brings. I used to work to make money to live, now I work to make money to feed my omnivorous habit. Sex, drugs, porn, alcohol, gambling, manic type-A personality, never-ending anxieties, rampant narcissism, or [fill in your own blank here] squat at the center of my solar system, and all my emotional energies revolve around it.

The question of who's really running your life is not as easy as it first sounds. You can declare your allegiance to Jesus Christ with all sincerity, yet still be emotionally enslaved to a hornet's nest of little tyrants playing tug of war with the scepter of your life.

Who's running your life?

I have good news for you from a God who's better than you think he is.

You Reign

When you became a Christian, in that very moment, God wrested the scepter of your life from all those nasty little dictators, and set it firmly and forever in your hands.

He gave you your dominion back.

What Adam lost in the Fall, Jesus Christ regained in the Redemption.

Who runs your life?

You do, under the mighty Lordship of Jesus Christ.

Say it with me: "I HAVE DOMINION."

Those fallen forces of your messy past don't own you. Those schoolyard labels don't define you. Those self-defeating habits don't rule you. Those nasty voices don't dominate you.

When Jesus shed his blood and rose from the grave, he crushed the opposition. In ancient warfare, the conquering king made his victory complete by performing a humiliating act against his defeated foe. In a great display put on for the soldiers and the nation, the conquering king trotted out the defeated king, threw him to the ground, and crushed his foe's head into the dirt with his foot.

Victory complete.

Scepter owned.

It's with this practice in mind that St. Paul wrote these words: "And the God of peace will crush Satan under YOUR feet shortly..." (Romans 16:20, emphasis added). The victory has already been completed – Jesus did that by his Cross. It's only a matter of time before one day you see with your own eyes the final consummation of Satan's ultimate defeat, with your very own foot crushing his creepy little head.

Until that day, you "reign in life" (Romans 5:17), says St. Paul. You, not the manipulative mutineers, captain your ship.

Here's a huge secret that so many Christians never really grasp: the dark forces in your life have no power but what you give them.

Jesus said, "All power is given unto me in heaven and in earth" (Matthew 28:18, KJV). All authority is his. All must bow before him, even the wackos. Even the bad guys. He rules. He reigns. He has dominion.

Because you are in union with Christ, guess what you share?

Dominion.

The scepter is in your hand. Dominion is yours. Where you steer the ship of your life is up to you. And if any creepy little usurpers try to run your life, control your life, define your life, or dominate your life, rise up to your full stature as the God-ordained sovereign of your life, and tell them to go take a flying leap, in Christian love.

It's time to recognize when you surrender the scepter to the crazies.

It's time to take your authority back.

The Fight

Like most Christians you've probably realized that the crazy forces in your life actually enjoy their phony dominion. They'll do anything to persuade you they own it by rights. Don't fall for it.

If you're going to regain your dominion, you have to embrace three great truths:

Truth one: *I take one hundred percent responsibility for my life and for my happiness right now.* No more blaming. Refuse to blame your pathetic life on your spouse, your ex-, the Man, the nasty DNA monsters inside you, the Big Guy Upstairs, or the horned guy downstairs.

If I could sit with you over coffee right now, and listen to all the trials you've faced, I'd do my best to show Christian compassion. But before we were finished swirling biscotti in our half-carafe-double-caff-cap, I would look you in the eye and tell you, from this moment onward, *you are nobody's victim.*

Peel off that *victim* label and run it through the shredder.

You may have been victimized in the past – hurt and wounded in incomprehensible ways. You may routinely call to mind horrendous scenes of helplessness and despair. My heart aches with you. It's brutally hard to rise above the horrible traumas of the past.

But you must.

And, by grace, you can.

My prayer for you today is that you would shed once for all the threadbare mantle of victimhood, that you might wrap around your shoulders the gleaming mantle of dominion.

It's time to take your scepter back, and that will not happen while you define your core self as a victim.

You may need counseling. You may need therapy. You may need meds. You may need to contact the authorities. You will definitely need time and prayer and growth and Scripture and trustworthy supporters.

But you can do this. You can take back your power. And it starts when you accept one hundred percent responsibility for the quality of your life from here on out. No excuses. No blaming. No lashing out. No wimping out.

Truth two: *I captain my ship under the mighty Lordship of Christ.* It's a subtle, but sanctified, form of wimping out – in some cases – to say, "I'm just seeking God's will." Before you throw the rotten tomatoes at me for what you suspect is heresy, let me explain.

Sometimes, God lets you choose whatever you want. He's good with multiple options in your life. Not always, but sometimes. Plenty of times. There are many times when God's perfect will for your life leaves room for your choice.

David declared, "Delight yourself also in the LORD, / And He shall give you the desires of your heart" (Psalm 37:4). Notice: the desires of your heart. When you delight in God, he opens doors for you to follow your heart.

As a college student, I was frequently stumped trying to find God's will for my life. Should I choose this major or that? Should I take this job or that? Should I date or wait? The questions were mounting for me, and I often felt paralyzed by indecision, afraid to make the wrong move. Then, I'd be stuck with God's "second best."

In fact, a saying was common in my little church: "Satan offers his second best before God offers his best."

Can you see how that would play with my mind? Especially when I was trying to make life-choices that pleased God? The consequence was paralysis by analysis. I couldn't be sure what God wanted, so I chose nothing. I didn't choose a major. I didn't choose a career. I didn't choose a mate. I was afraid that I would turn left when God wanted me to turn right, and then I'd be stuck in life's cheap seats forever.

Somehow, I grabbed a copy of a book that changed my life. It became an instant classic: *Decision-Making and the Will of God,* by Gary Friesen[8].

Friesen compared the traditional view of God's will with trying to hit a bulls-eye. Miss the center, and you could be stuck with a second rate life forever. That was exactly the stress I was feeling.

He suggested a different model. Based in part on Psalm 37:4, he suggested that instead of thinking *bulls-eye,* we should think *yard.* God offers parameters in Scripture, like fences around a big, beautiful yard. Within those parameters, there may be multiple, valid, biblically permissible, options. When that happens, *choose whichever one you want most.*

Freisen was right. You have dominion for exactly this reason: to captain the ship of your life, within biblical parameters, wherever you darn well please.

Take the scepter back, and choose the life you really want – the truest, deepest life of your dreams. The life you hope for on your best days.

Because that's when the third great truth comes into play: *wherever I may steer the ship, God goes with me.* He doesn't say, "You were supposed to turn left there instead of right, so I'm abandoning you now. You were supposed to go to that other college, or accept that other job or marry that other person, so from now on you're on your own."

Never.

Instead, God engraved this enduring promise on the pages of Scripture:

> And the LORD, He is the one who goes before you. He will be with you, He will not leave you nor forsake

you; do not fear nor be dismayed. (Deuteronomy 31:8)

When you exercise your dominion with faith in God and a willingness to stay between the lines Scripture draws, you can't go wrong. Your greatest blessing, your highest potential, and your God-given dreams are ensured by the personal presence of God himself.

God will even go with you in the wrong turns. However, those wrong turns will most often hurt. When you break your promises, when you slog through sin, or when you violate Scripture's truths, you frustrate yourself. You beat your head against the bedrock of God's reality. You introduce inner contradictions your soul can't bear. You generate needless drama faster than a nuclear reactor spews forth toxins.

Worst of all, you run crossways to Christ's beautiful life in you.

So, keep your commitments, honor your marriage, date with integrity, grow mature in Christ, rear your children faithfully, respect your spouse, be a person of your word, be wise – in other words, obey Scripture. Within these parameters, you will find your highest and truest life by following your heart.

Yes, that's how much dominion you have. You have Christ in you. You rule. Wield the scepter with joy.

Love God, said Augustine, and do what you want.

Now go out and design a realm better than your wildest dreams.

Additional Scriptures

Psalm 37:4, Romans 5:17, 1 Chronicles 4:10, Revelation 1:6; 5:10.

Prayer

My Lord,

You reign over all things. You are the mighty sovereign of the cosmic realms. I bow before you to say that your dominion stretches over all things, great and small. You are my King, my God, my Lord, and my everything.

How I thank you today for sharing with me your mighty dominion. I bless you for wresting the scepter from every dark force, and returning it to me. I claim my authority, under you. I stand in my true power.

I declare my life and my realm to be off limits to the powers of evil. Dysfunction does not rule me. Other people's craziness does not define me. Death and hell have no dominion over me. Sin's power is broken. Addiction, despair, curses, and ill will cannot dominate me. I reign in life today. I hold the scepter. I captain my life under the mighty Lordship of you, Almighty King.

Lord, where I have surrendered my power to foolishness, I take it back today.

Whatever turf I have yielded to unrighteousness and sin, I now yield back to you.

My habits and thoughts of weakness and fear, I turn into strength and victory in Jesus' name.

I will not wimp out, lash out, or cave in. I will operate in the quiet strength of my utterly secure royalty.

Show me my deepest wants, within the parameters of your perfect Word, and give me the courage to boldly go wherever my heart may lead.

I will exercise dominion to the glory of your name. I will exercise dominion for the blessing of my world. I will exercise dominion for the joy of my own heart. I will maintain healthy boundaries. I will not be bossed around, and I will not boss others around.

I take one hundred percent responsibility for my life. Lord, I am nobody's victim. I have dominion. Help me rise above the painful memories of the past.

Thank you for going with me wherever I may turn. Help me to honor each person I see today.

In Jesus' Name,

Amen.

CHAPTER 19

I HAVE A SUPERPOWER

Meditation

It is urgently needful that the Christian people of our charge should come to understand that they are not a company of invalids, to be wheeled about, or fed by hand, cosseted, nursed, and comforted, the minister being the Head Physician and Nurse; but a garrison in an enemy's country, every soul of which should have some post of duty, at which he should be prepared to make any sacrifice rather than quitting. ~F. B. Meyer, 1800s

Scripture

"For as we have many members in one body, but all the members do not have the same function, so we, being many, are one body in Christ, and individually members of one another. Having then gifts differing according to the grace that is given to us, let us use them: if prophecy, let us prophesy in proportion to our faith; or ministry, let us use it in our ministering; he who teaches, in teaching; he who exhorts, in exhortation; he who gives, with liberality; he who leads, with diligence; he who shows mercy, with cheerfulness." (Romans 12:4-8)

Bible Study

IT'S TIME TO CLAIM YOUR superpower. I've said from the beginning that if you are a Christian, you are in permanent union with Jesus Christ. You are in him, and he is in you.

One practical way this works out in your life is through a package of internal motivations called "spiritual gifts." Paul speaks of Christians "having gifts differing" from one another (Romans 12:6). He then lists seven different spiritual gifts: prophecy, service, teaching, exhortation, giving, leading, and mercy. There are other lists of gifts in other places in the Bible (Ephesians 4 and 1 Corinthians 12, 1 Peter), but this is enough for a start.

Notice the variety. Imagine a football team running onto the field, and every player wants to be quarterback. That's a sure plan for a crushing defeat. Or, as a chef, imagine a stew in which every line cook added the same ingredient and the same spice: carrots and cayenne pepper times ten.

No thank you.

So it is within the church, the body of Christ. In order for us to represent Jesus in the world – to be his arms to embrace, his hands to serve, his feet to go, his wallet to give, his ear to listen, his shoulder to cry upon, his mouth to speak – he has given every Christian a unique package of spiritual gifts.

Nobody is just like you. You have a superpower – a one of a kind, grace-given, supernaturally empowered mix of abilities and passions.

Your spiritual gifts are like an internal circuit board from heaven. They motivate your Christian service. They help you serve Christ and his kingdom. They enable you to sparkle in this service. When you serve God in ways that align with your gifts, you feel like you've plugged into an endless source of energy. When you serve God in ways that don't match your spiritual gifts, you get tired and frustrated. When you operate within your giftings, the Holy Spirit brings forth much fruit. Lives are changed. The church is blessed. The on-looking world witnesses the gospel of grace in a whole new way.

As a preacher, and as a preaching professor, I've seen many people who have stars in their eyes about preaching. But they have no gifts for preaching, so when they try it, it's brutal. They're not happy. Their listeners aren't happy. Nobody's happy till it's over. The key is to find your gift – discover your particular God-given wiring – and then direct your service to God down those avenues.

That doesn't mean you can be like a snooty employee turning your back when a need arises: "Sorry, not my union." No, pitch in and lend a hand even if it's not your gift.

But your life should mainly tell the story of serving Christ and his kingdom through your superpower.

A Gifted Tribe

When God told Moses to build the tabernacle (a massive tent for worship), there were specific leaders with specific gifts to do different parts of the project. God raised up an artisan named Bazalel, and said:

"I have filled him with the Spirit of God, in wisdom, in understanding, in knowledge, and in all manner of workmanship, to design artistic works, to work in gold, in silver, in bronze, in cutting jewels for setting, in carving wood, and to work in all manner of workmanship." (Exodus 31:1-5)

Bezalel was wired for artistic craftsmanship. Aholiab, in the next paragraph of Exodus, was wired for making beautiful, artistic furnishings.

They were different.

When they worked together, the results sparkled.

I am wired to serve God a certain way – mainly through preaching and teaching, whether I write it or speak it out loud. I also have a gift of leadership and can galvanize action in a certain direction.

None of this makes me superior. I can't boast of these things. These are *gifts*. All I can do is look to God and say thank you.

Nor does this necessarily make me good at what I do. I still have to study. I have to master my craft. I have devoured over a hundred books on preaching. I study preachers. I read classic sermons. I take in feedback. I train my preaching muscles to run the marathon of my life's work, working, by God's grace, to be a well-prepared preacher. When it comes to ministry, the grace isn't just in the delivery; it's in the preparation too.

Your superpower will limp along without dedicated training. It's less like a magic wand, and more like enhanced DNA for certain spiritual muscles.

You still have to train.

You have your own set of gifts, different than mine. It's only when we work together that our superpowers really sparkle. And that's when your service to God meshes with mine to truly help people find and follow God.

Like I said, I'm a preacher. I can't flex my superpower muscles without hundreds of other people flexing theirs. Some are most happy setting up seats and cleaning the bathrooms. Some embrace other people's children, giving worn out parents a chance to hear God's Word. Others keep our church's financial books honest and our bills paid on time. Yet others operate microphones, provide an atmosphere of worship, and ensure the air-conditioners keep our worship space from turning into a sauna.

God insists his people act like a body, and our superpowers work synergistically to punch holes through the devil's stupid lies.

God has assembled a rag-tag group of followers into an unstoppable force called the Church. Each of us, in union with Christ, and working together, can do magic in our corner of this bedraggled planet. Together, through our gifts, we bring Jesus to the world, and the world to him.

Discovering Your Superpower

Here are five simple steps to discover your unique mix of spiritual gifts.

1. Get involved. Plug into a ministry. Take a short-term missions trip. Do community service. Almost every church needs help in the children's ministry. Spend a summer serving God's favorite people: kids. Volunteer inside or outside the church. Your superpower rears its beautiful head only as you serve Christ and his kingdom. But remember, we never serve God *for* blessing; we only serve him *from* blessing.

2. Notice your energy. As you serve, be aware of your energy. Jesus said "his yoke was easy and his burden was light" (Matthew 11:30). If there's a mismatch between your service and your superpower, everything will feel like a chore. But when you're in the gift zone, ministry hardly feels like work. You'll find joy. You'll be glad you're there. You'll love it. Of course, you will get tired. When I was in kids' ministries, I started each fall with super high energy. Come spring, the summer break couldn't come fast enough. Those seasons are normal. But overall, your spiritual gift is jet fuel for your service for Christ. Pay attention.

3. Look for fruit. Also, pay attention to the results of your ministry. The great preacher, Charles Spurgeon, criticized some preachers for having "the gift of dispersion." Instead of gathering congregations, they sent them scrambling for the exits. When you operate within your gift mix, you will usually see positive results. People will be saved. Ministries will grow. Families will be blessed, encouraged, thankful. The Holy Spirit will swoop down, and Christ within will bear much fruit through you. If you are involved in fruitless ministry, check your calling from God and double-check if your gifts match you for this type of service.

A special word to those who would be pastors: Conventional wisdom says if you can see yourself being happy doing anything else, then do it. Conventional wisdom is right. There is something about the stature, the status, the God-closeness, the microphone, the adulation that ignites pastoral stars in the eyes of career-seekers. Don't buy the myth. Pastoring is brutally hard work for reasons you wouldn't expect, even with properly matched superpowers. It is impossible to thrive without the right gifts.

I had a friend who dreamed of being a pastor. He was a car mechanic, who decided to take Greek classes at a local seminary. The classes slayed him. He hated every minute of it and was failing. I suggested that seeing him in Greek class made as much sense to me as Mike Ditka (former head coach of the Chicago Bears, and all around tough guy) in a tutu. Another friend pressed through college to a ministry degree, but every ministry she ever had shrank to oblivion.

Look for fruit.

4. *Seek honest confirmation.* Listen to feedback from others – except from your mom. Have you heard of American Idol Syndrome? No? Well, I just made it up. It's what happens when moms gush over their tone-deaf children's' off-pitch caterwauling. For seventeen years, they lie. "Honey, that was beautiful! You should be a singer!" Other family and friends, too nice to tell the truth, add their praise. The kid grows up thinking he can sing. It's not until he finally auditions before Harry Connick Jr. that he hears the awful truth: "Buddy,

singing is not for you." When you serve God with your superpower, Christ-in-you shines and others see it. Yes, we all have growing to do in our gifts, but serving God is *natural* for Christ, and so it is natural for those whom he indwells – so beautifully natural that others stand and cheer. Listen to the testimony of the body of Christ.

5. *Don't give up.* If one ministry doesn't suit you, finish out your commitment, and try something else. Go for variety. Serve. Speak. Counsel. Teach. Set up chairs. Equipment. Clean the kitchen. Get dirty. Go. Stay. Adults. Kids. Seniors. Cross-cultural. Give. Give some more. Exit the familiar, push your boundaries, experiment. Something will click with you. You will feel it. The church will see it. God will cheer it. And you will fly.

Additional Scriptures

Romans 12:5-8, 1 Corinthians 12:4-11; 27-31, Ephesians 4:11,12, 1 Peter 4:10,11.

Prayer

Dear Giver of All Good Things,
Others may see little of value in me, but you see the great treasure you have deposited deep within. Thank you. My spirit rises up to say, "I am gifted. I am enabled. I have a superpower." I confess I've been slinking in the shadows, when you created me to soar. You made me to serve and to tend the garden of this world. You made me to shine in my arena of ministry. I am not here just for my own blessing – though I'm thankful for that – but I'm here to transmit your mind-blowing blessings to others. I can't wait!

Help me, Lord, to discover my gifts. Give me strength and joy in the journey. For every step I take into the scary realm of service for you, add your strength, add your motivation, and grant that I might see much fruit for my grace-inspired labors.

I want nothing more than to be used by you, dear Father, for Christ and his kingdom. I seek the privilege of being part of your great global project of drawing lost sinners to yourself and making them whole in you. I want to help people find and follow you. Grant that I would do that with passion, energy, and excellence that can only come through Christ in me.

Thank you for entrusting me with the gospel.

Help me share it well, in my own world and ways.

In Christ's Name,

Amen.

CHAPTER 20

I AM DELIVERED FROM DARKNESS

Meditation

Nothing can overturn the mind which abides in faith. Nothing can destroy me which does not first unsettle and destroy my faith. While I continue to believe, I am secure against every danger. Faith in God meets every charge and every foe with perfect success. Does conscience accuse? Faith reveals divine forgiveness in the blood of Christ. Does the law condemn? Faith proclaims everlasting righteousness in the obedience of Christ. Does the world persecute or tempt? Faith assures of triumphant protection in the power of Christ. Does Satan threaten? Faith announces unlimited victory in the kingdom of Christ. Faith meets every objection. It says, "Only believe—all things are possible to him that believes." ~Stephen Tyng, 1800s

Scripture

He has delivered us from the power of darkness and conveyed us into the kingdom of the Son of His love. (Colossians 1:13)

Inasmuch then as the children have partaken of flesh and blood, He Himself likewise shared in the same, that through death He might destroy him who had the power of death, that is, the devil, and release those who through fear of death were all their lifetime subject to bondage. (Hebrews 2:14, 15)

Bible Study

DEMONIC POWERS, EVIL SPELLS, curses, and bad horoscopes are no match for the humblest saint robed in the righteousness of Christ. You may have sprung from a cursed family tree, but those curses were broken the instant you were joined to Christ.

The Bible tells of another realm of existence, greater than this one we can see, permeating it, and all around it. It is a realm of angels and demons, heaven and hell, God and the devil. The great battle of the ages rolls on, but with one unimpeachable certainty:

Christ triumphs over all.

He has triumphed over every dark force, once for all. That includes the devil. That includes the demons. That includes the insanity bug that gnawed its way from branch to branch on your dysfunctional family tree. Christ smashed it into a gooey little mess.

In Christ: you > the devil.

Christians need not fear any dark power. Christ is your shield, your defender, your fortress, and your strong tower. No weapon can defeat him, so no weapon of darkness can defeat you.

Superstition has no hold on you. The evil eye, bad luck, and karma have no power over you. Fortune tellers, horoscopes, Ouija boards, palm readers, and tarot cards have nothing to say to you. Why would you open your soul's door to those foul odors? Respect yourself enough, and respect God enough, to tune into the voice of God alone through Scripture alone.

Scripture declares you have been delivered out from the powers of darkness. The devil's dark domain may sputter and fume, but it's all bluster. Don't be fooled. Don't be frightened. In Christ, you have all the power you need to stand victorious.

We've already seen your dominion.

We've already cheered the promise that "the God of Peace will crush the devil's head under your foot shortly."

We've already rested in the triumph of Christ's glorious resurrection.

Now, it's time to rest your anxious thoughts within the arms of his almighty victory.

He embarrassed the devil. He routed the demons. He humiliated them, putting them all to open shame. The Bible declares: "Having disarmed principalities and powers, He made a public spectacle of them, triumphing over them in it" (Colossians 2:15). Three cheers for the winning side.

Does this mean the dark side means nothing to you?

No.

The war is real, the devil won't quit. His primary way of getting to you is through the lies you believe. His evil lies permeate society. Like counterfeit money, the devil's deceptions lure many astray. If he can get you to believe his lies – mainly about how you label yourself and God – then he can at least neutralize you in the ongoing cosmic battle for supremacy.

How can you stand strong?

Wear Your Armor

You'll find no better Grace Rehab instructions against the devil's dark domain than Paul's exhortation to wear your spiritual armor:

> Finally, my brethren, be strong in the Lord and in the power of His might. Put on the whole armor of God, that you may be able to stand against the wiles of the devil. For we do not wrestle against flesh and blood, but against principalities, against powers, against the rulers of the darkness of this age, against spiritual hosts of wickedness in the heavenly places. Therefore take up the whole armor of God, that you may be able to withstand in the evil day, and having done all, to stand. Stand therefore, having girded your waist with truth, having put on the breastplate of righteousness, and having shod your feet with the preparation of the gospel of peace; above all, taking the shield of faith with which you will be able to quench all the fiery darts of the wicked one. And take the helmet of salvation, and the sword of the Spirit, which is the word of God... (Ephesians 6:10-17)

When I coached my son's Pee Wee football team, at start time we'd blow our whistles and tell the players to "gear up." The players scrambled to put on helmets and pads so they could deliver a hit. God tells you to gear up too. In one sense, that's what this entire book has been about. We're putting on the whole armor of God. We're wrapping ourselves in the invincible armor of who we are in Christ. We're displacing the doctrines of demons with the doctrines of grace, the devil's lies with God's truth. We're renewing our minds, reformatting our hard drives, and installing omnipotent grace as our permanent operating system.

You can stand strong in Christ.

You don't have to cower before the dark side.

The victory is yours.

Believe it and do not be afraid.

Additional Scriptures

Ephesians 2:1-10, Acts 26:18, Romans 8:37, 1 Peter 3:22, 1 Corinthians 10:4,5.

Prayer

Almighty Father,

I stand in your victory today. I cheer your Son's glorious triumph over every dark force. He routed the devil. He put to shame the demons. He exposed the devil's lies, and dragged that wily enemy into the blistering light of invincible truth. In Christ, I find my strength, my victory, and my triumph.

As I walk in your ways, trusting your Word...

...I believe no weapon formed against me will prosper.

...I declare all who rise against me will fall.

I am a warrior, but my weapons are not of the flesh – they are mighty through God. They are the words and truths, the promises and principles, the doctrines and realities of your precious Word. With these, I slay the devil's lies. With your truth, I defeat my own insecurities. I rise above them as a Christian in complete armor, clothed in Christ and his almighty strength.

The gospel is still the power of God!

I label myself, "More than a conqueror!"

I may feel afraid, but I won't let fear rule my life. The massive forces of darkness have no say in my life. I spit out bad luck, bad karma, bad juju, and bad anything. I call out the

horoscope, Ouija board, fortune-teller, and palm reader as liars,
and I anchor my soul in the truth of God alone.

My hope is in Christ, who triumphed over the devil and spanked
his nasty minions into retreat.

With faith in my heart, and Christ in my life, victory is assured.

I am more than a conqueror through Christ, my Lord,

In Whose Name I Pray,

Amen.

CHAPTER 21

I AM AN HEIR OF GOD

Meditation

With such a glorious inheritance reserved for God's children, what are earth's pomps and vanities? How do its riches, and honors, and ambitions pale into utter nothingness before the approaching blaze of that advent throne! ~John MacDuff, 1874

Scripture

[A]nd if children, then heirs – heirs of God and joint heirs with Christ... (Romans 8:17)

Therefore you are no longer a slave but a son, and if a son, then an heir of God through Christ. (Galatians 4:7)

Bible Study

THE NAMES JIM, JOHN, ALICE, AND ROBSON might mean little to you, but odds are strong you've bought their stuff. Their father, Sam Walton, founded the Walmart megastores, and upon his passing in 1992, his four children inherited a staggering $135 billion estate.

As rich as that estate might be, it pales in comparison to your inheritance in Christ. Long before this beautiful world sprang from the hand of God, before he spun the planets into their orbits, and hung the galaxies into space, long before angels, and energy and matter and the space-time continuum, there was our Triune God alone.

In his eternal councils, God decided to bring our universe into being. Along with that, he determined to create us – the human race – in his own image. God knew what would happen. He knew we would sin. He knew we would need a Savior.

The Father devised the plan of salvation.

The Son implemented the plan, signing up to be that Savior.

The Spirit energized the plan, empowering Christ in his time on earth, and revealing his saving work to the world of humankind.

The whole Trinity brought about our awesome salvation.

Here's where a wonderful truth comes in. To honor the Son for his work of salvation, the Father made him a promise. God promised to pour out on Jesus Christ all the wealth of the cosmos.

> [God] has in these last days spoken to us by *His* Son, whom He has appointed heir of all things, through whom also He made the worlds. (Hebrews 1:2)

God has appointed him "heir of all things." All things. That is the ancient way of referring to the cosmos and everything within it. It means the whole universe.

Jesus Christ inherits it all. Everything. Every gold nugget, every silver vein, every sparkling diamond, every coin and currency. He inherits properties. He inherits lands. He inherits buildings and skyscrapers and mansions and yachts. Nations are his. Kingdoms are his. Armies are his. Ranches, forests, and farms are his.

If it has a moving molecule of matter, Christ claims it. If it has a sizzling spark of energy, it's his. From the farthest star in the remotest galaxy, to the tiniest life form in the deepest sea, there's not anything, anywhere, in all of time and eternity that isn't the property of the Lord Jesus Christ as the rightful heir of all things.

> The LORD has said to Me, 'You *are* My Son, Today I have begotten You. Ask of Me, and I will give *You* The nations *for* Your inheritance, And the ends of the earth *for* Your possession. (Psalm 2:7, 8)

Let's take ourselves out of the picture for a moment. Let's just think about God. Just God.

Christianity begins and ends with Jesus Christ. World history is nothing but the story of God the Father and God the Holy Spirit preparing to pour out the treasures of the universe on the Lord Jesus Christ.

It's awesome to contemplate.

But here's where it gets even more awesome.

Joint Heirs

People say all religions are the same.

People are right, if by religion they mean a system that binds people to duty, obligation, performance, and payment in order to merit the favor of God. Ugh! That gigantic hamster wheel of religion takes a thousand different forms. In the end, it truly is all one thing: salvation by works. Humans reaching up to God.

Yes, religions are all the same in the ceaseless struggle to earn a paycheck from an impossible-to-please divine Employer.

But there is one system, and only one, that stands completely outside the religious system. It is the un-religion. It's not about humans reaching up; it's about God reaching down. Not about an Employer to work for but a Savior who, at unspeakable cost, did a work for us on Calvary's cross to purchase in full the salvation we could never earn.

Not a religion, but a gospel. Not works, but grace. There is only one gospel: the good news of Jesus Christ. This message sets Christianity in a league of its own.

The good news we proclaim says that when you put your simple faith in Christ – apart from any works you have done – God joins you to Christ. As he is the heir of all things, you become a joint heir with him of all things (Romans 8:17, 32). As the moving molecules and sizzling sparks and currencies and coins are all his, so they become yours too.

Remarkable to think of it. Unparalleled in the annals of religion. God blesses exactly One Person with an eternal inheritance. You, by faith, are joined to the One Person. You share his inheritance forever. What a salvation!

Exactly how do we become joint heirs with Jesus? Not by our many good works, but by Christ's singular finished work at the Cross. God calls these treasures our *inheritance* because somebody had to die for us to get them.

Now when someone dies and leaves a will, no one gets anything until it is proved that the person who wrote the will is dead. The will goes into effect only after the death of the person who wrote it. While the person is still alive, no one can use the will to get any of the things promised to them. (Hebrews 9:16, 17, NLT)

Once again, the Word of God directs us with laser beam focus to the Cross of Christ. It is his death that activates the "last will and testament" of God.

When I was a kid in Sunday School, I sang this little chorus:

> He owns the cattle on a thousand hills,
> The wealth in every mine!
> He owns the rivers and the rocks and rills,
> The sun and stars that shine!
> Wonderful riches, more than tongue can tell,
> He is my Father so they're mine as well!
> He owns the cattle on a thousand hills,
> I know that he will care for me![9]

"They're mine as well."

The next time you're tempted to label yourself poor, afflicted, and alone, remind yourself of who you are. You're a joint heir with Jesus and your glory is veiled in your meager earthly frame. One day, you will come into your full inheritance.

Until then, you have a blank check to claim all you need through prayer. Until then, you walk by faith with the easy confidence of the world's richest heir.

Additional Scriptures

1 Peter 1:4, Acts 20:32, Ephesians 1:11-14, Titus 3:7

Prayer

Gracious Lord,

It's hard to believe that you call me a joint heir with Jesus Christ. But you do, so I accept that label.

I bless you, Jesus, as rightful heir of all things. The starry cosmos and everything it contains is yours. The wealth of nations. The glory of earth's kingdoms. I declare that all things are yours by right and by redemption. How I long for that glorious day when the treasures of creation will be poured at your feet.

I am astounded to know that I will share that blessing with you. My name is written alongside yours, Lord Jesus, on the deed to the heavenly vault. I can't wait to step into my eternal inheritance with you.

Until that day, I walk by faith and not by sight.

I believe you are meeting all my needs, day by day.

And I trust that, from my heavenly portfolio of assets, you will never let my earthly provision run dry.

Help me to see the great potential in each person I meet today.

Through Christ I pray,

Amen.

CHAPTER 22

I AM BEING SANCTIFIED

Meditation

Sanctification is the gift of the Holy Spirit, the fruit of the Spirit, the grace of the Lord Jesus Christ and the prepared inheritance of all who enter in. It is the obtainment of faith, not the attainment of works. It is divine holiness, not human self-improvement or perfection. It is the inflow into man's being of the life and purity of the infinite, eternal and Holy One. It is the bringing in of God's own perfection and the working out of His own will. How easy, how spontaneous, how delightful this heavenly way of holiness! Surely it is a "highway" and not the low way of man's vain and fruitless mortification. It is God's great elevated railway, sweeping over the heads of the struggling throngs who toil along the lower road when they might be borne along on His ascension pathway by His own almighty impulse. It is God's great elevator carrying us up to the higher chambers of His palace, without arduous efforts, while others struggle up the winding stairs and faint by the way. ~A.B. Simpson, 1800s

Scripture

By that will we have been sanctified through the offering of the body of Jesus Christ once for all. Hebrews 10:10

For by one offering He has perfected forever those who are being sanctified. Hebrews 10:14

Bible Study

I OFFERED TWO BIBLE VERSES in today's Scripture section. Both of them speak of sanctification, which I'll explain a bit more in a moment. Notice the *tenses* of their verbs. Hebrews 10:10 says *we have been* sanctified, in the past tense, as a once for all deal. Hebrews 10:14 says *we are being* sanctified, in the present tense, as an ongoing, every day reality. The Author of Hebrews had no problem putting these two aspects of sanctification into one tight paragraph. Why the two tenses?

The massive emphasis of your entire Grace Rehab depends on you getting a grip on what God has done for you, decisively, once for all, in the past tense, through Jesus Christ crucified and risen again. The demeaning labels, the humiliating slurs, and the cruel insults that the world has slapped on you have all been erased in Jesus Christ. The first part of your soul's recovery consists of driving hundreds of doctrinal/biblical anchor-bolts into the bedrock of God's absolute acceptance of you in Christ.

You have been "perfected forever" in the eyes of God. That is your past tense truth.

Now, in the present tense, God works daily to emblazon that reality across your feelings and experience, and before the eyes of a desperately lost world.

So you have a salvation – and a sanctification, redemption, and everything else – in two tenses.

Make that three. I first learned these tenses when I was an eight-year-old boy in the kids' club, called Awana, at my church. Over the years, I have seen how much clarity they bring to the Bible's message. I'm so thankful I learned these early in my Christian life. Here they are.

Salvation in Three Time Zones

1. Past Tense: Salvation from the PENALTY of Sin.

This is your forgiveness, your justification, and your initial redemption, all wrapped as Christ's great gift, and given to you in full the moment you first believed. As a past tense reality, your salvation sparkles as a once for all done deal – signed, sealed, and delivered – with a finality and perfection only Christ can achieve. This is the tense we've been dwelling on throughout this book. It's crucial, because these truths define you. They create your identity. They energize everything else that happens in your life with God.

2. Present Tense: Salvation from the POWER of Sin.

This is the ongoing work of God through Christ in you, by the power of the Holy Spirit. The present tense work of God is usually called *sanctification*. It's tricky, because *sanctification* is used in both the past tense – so it's a finished work of God (Hebrews 10:10) – and also in the present tense – so it's an ongoing work of God (Hebrews 10:14). In each case, you have to let the context of the Bible verse help you interpret which time zone the biblical author has in mind.

When Scripture says you are being sanctified, in the present tense, it unveils an important clue to your ongoing Grace Rehab. Let me mention salvation's third tense, and then come back to this.

3. Future Tense: Salvation from the PRESENCE of Sin.

Future tense sanctification is heaven. All the messy stuff will vanish away. Light will displace the darkness. Purity will shove out temptation. Joy will overwhelm sorrows. There is coming a day when sin won't even be the tiniest speck of lint on your imagination's lapel. In that day, you will be who you really are, to the maximum, not only in your status, but in your experience too.

These three tenses – past, present, and future – map out the entire journey of your life with God. I'd like to spend the rest of this chapter focusing on sanctification in the present tense.

You Are Being Sanctified

To be sanctified means to be holy. Sanctification is the process by which God makes you holy in your present tense lifestyle on planet earth.

A good golf swing has a smooth follow through, and God's good work of justification has a smooth follow through too: present tense sanctification. The righteous life of you in Christ morphs into the righteous lifestyle of Christ in you.

Your legal and mystical unions with Christ bear fruit in the moral union (see Part One for what this means).

It is by sanctification that you stop cussing, quit looking at porn, zip your gossiping lip, and bite your critical tongue. Sanctification delivers you from a life of self-serving narcissism. By it, you become a generous person. A functional soul. A good and kind friend. A faithful spouse. You become morally pure and relationally whole. You develop staying power, endurance through tough times with dignity and grace.

Sanctification makes you a good ambassador of Christ and enables you to contribute your life to God's great work of drawing a lost world to the Savior.

Your friends see Jesus and scratch their heads over what makes you tick.

Sanctification is God's way of unburying the real you from the lifetime of crud you've accumulated. It peels off the ugly labels and unleashes your truest self. It makes you the person you always dreamed of becoming, overflowing with love, and wholeness, and goodness, and grace.

A sanctified Christian serves God and bears much fruit.

A sanctified Christian changes the world.

The cherry on the sundae of a sanctified soul is the beautiful quality called love. Just as a football team drives toward the end zone, so sanctification drives toward love. A mature, 1 Corinthians 13 style love shines forever as the epitome of your Christian life.

Sanctification, therefore, makes you like Christ.

And that is a good thing.

It is also a miracle.

And this is where most Christians get it wrong.

A Miracle of Grace

True sanctification requires the supernatural power of God. It is a mistake to think you are saved by God but then sanctified by works. Or by yourself alone. No. You're not strong enough to do sanctification's heavy lifting. Your bad habits are too strong. Your selfish streak runs too deep. Your self-talk and the decisions that follow are simply too insane for you to fix by your own power. Life's ugly labels won't come off by human strength alone. You are not strong enough.

But Christ is.

And that is why he moved into you at salvation. He's the one flexing his almighty biceps to work out sanctification in your otherwise decrepit life. The Bible makes this super-clear:

> Therefore, my beloved, as you have always obeyed, not as in my presence only, but now much more in my absence, work out your own salvation with fear and trembling; for it is God who works in you both to will and to do for His good pleasure. (Philippians 2:12, 13)

I have to point out that legalists love to bash Christians on the head with the first part of this Scripture, while ignoring the second. You do not produce your sanctification, God does. He works in you in such a way that you both, a) have the desire or will, and, b) actually do "his good pleasure." That's God's work. That's God's good work in you. You work out what he worked in. Like working out the giant shoelace that got pulled out of your hoodie: you didn't make it, you just work to the surface what somebody else produced.

That explains why one of God's self-given labels is Yahweh Meqaddesh (muh-cod-DESH), The Lord Who Sanctifies. "You shall not profane My holy name, but I will be hallowed among the children of Israel. I am the LORD who sanctifies you" (Leviticus 22:32). On your good days you will admit you're such a mess it requires a miracle of divine grace to clean you up.

So Paul declares his confidence "that He who has begun a good work in you will complete it until the day of Jesus Christ" (Philippians 1:6). He began it on the day you were saved and won't quit till he beams you up to heaven.

If you want to drive yourself crazy, picture sanctification as your responsibility. Strain and strive for a lifetime; you'll still come up short. You'll produce a false sanctification by human power. You'll impress your church friends, but not God. "God does not dwell in temples made with hands," and he does not make himself at home inside holiness made by human hands either (Acts 17:24).

If you want to lay hold of sanity and peace, cast the burden of your holiness on the Lord, and he will bring it to pass. He will exchange your brokenness for Christ's wholeness. He will prove himself in your everyday life as the Lord Who Sanctifies.

Hudson Taylor's Breakthrough

In the 1800s, a pioneer missionary to China named Hudson Taylor coined the phrase, "the exchanged life." He told the story of sweating and straining to be a better Christian. He prayed, fasted, studied, agonized, determined, vowed, labored, and went above and beyond the call of duty in order to please God as a missionary and a Christian. This continued over a long period of time.

It wore him out. And it didn't work. He never moved one inch closer to sanctification's end zone.

Taylor said, "I strove for faith, but it would not come; I tried to exercise it, but in vain. Seeing more and more the wondrous supply of grace laid up in Jesus, the fullness of our precious Saviour, my guilt and helplessness seemed to increase... What was I to do?"

If you've been around the Christian block a few times, you've probably shared a similar struggle. Hopefully you can share Taylor's breakthrough too.

A single line in a random letter from a friend exploded across his consciousness. Taylor said,

> When my agony of soul was at its height, a sentence in a letter from dear McCarthy was used to remove the scales from my eyes, and the Spirit of God revealed to me the truth of our oneness with Jesus as I had never known it before. "But how to get faith strengthened? Not by striving after faith, but by resting on the Faithful One."[10]

Not by striving, but by resting.
Not by my labors, but by Christ's faithfulness.

It was a breakthrough. Everything changed. Hudson Taylor went on to describe sanctification as an "exchanged life." The Exchanged Life title has taken hold, and is the most biblical way of understanding present-tense sanctification.

Another great church leader from the past described a similar breakthrough. Nineteenth century Pastor F.B. Meyer, whose books inhabit the shelves of many pastors even today, went through a similar period of striving and straining after sanctification. He described a very long prayer meeting in which he and others "agonized" in prayer for God to zap them with supernatural holiness. On his walk home that night, the Holy Spirit put together scriptural truth for him in a startlingly new way. Meyer wrote,

> I left the prayer meeting and crept away into the lane praying, 'O Lord, if there was ever a man who needs the power of the Holy Spirit, it is I. But I do not know how to receive Him; I am too tired, too worn, too nervously run down to agonize.' Then a voice said to me, 'As you took forgiveness from the hand of the dying Christ, take the Holy Spirit [in his sanctifying power] from the hand of the living Christ.'[11]

It was a dramatic moment of sanctification for him. Meyer wrote, "I took for the first time and have kept on taking ever since." Without emotion, feeling, or excitement – without any requirement but claiming it by faith alone, Meyer said – he simply trusted God to work out sanctification within him. And God proved faithful. Along with Hudson Taylor, F.B. Meyer found the Exchanged Life too. What is it?

What is the Exchanged Life?

The Exchanged Life is simply a title for a biblical picture of sanctification. It is most clearly stated in Galatians 2:20:

> I have been crucified with Christ; it is no longer I who live, but Christ lives in me; and the life which I now live in the flesh I live by faith in the Son of God, who loved me and gave Himself for me. (Galatians 2:20)

Your union with Christ joined you to his death, so you are "crucified with Christ." Even so, here you are, walking around on planet earth, looking very much alive. How does that work?

As we saw in chapter 4, the old you, You-Plus-Zero, is gone. That identity no longer roams the planet.

The new you, however, You-Plus-Christ, is very much alive. Your union with Christ actually means something in how you live your life. The Exchanged Life is the moral union in action.

So Christ lives *in* you. By living *in* you, he is able to live *through* you. He has taken onto himself all your bad stuff, and buried it in the deepest sea. He has added into you all the good stuff. For all your days, he will polish that good stuff till it shines like a Ferrari on the showroom floor.

Consider it a trade in which you get the [infinitely] better end of the deal. You exchange:

Your sins for Christ's righteousness.

Your weakness for Christ's strength.

Your poverty for Christ's unsearchable riches.

Your cursing for Christ's blessing.

Your bondage for Christ's freedom.

Your chaos for Christ's peace.

Your shame for Christ's glory.

Your guilt for Christ's holiness.

Your confusion for Christ's wisdom.

Your unholiness for Christ's sanctification.

Your "I can't" for Christ's "I can."

You make this exchange daily. Hourly. As often as you remember to do it. You make this exchange by faith, not by works. In grace-filled sanctification, you flip your emotional, mental, and spiritual switches from your efforts to Christ's.

When Taylor spoke of "resting" in Christ's faithfulness, he meant believing in each of these exchanges at just the right moment. For example, when you feel weak, that's the moment to rely upon Christ's strength. That is the precise moment when you consciously exchange your weakness for his strength – remembering from Chapter 17 that there is no official feeling of the power of God.

Or, when you are tempted to sin, in that very moment it's time to trade your sin for Christ's righteousness. When you find yourself in any situation on the left side of the Exchanged Life list, you need the mature faith to claim your birthright on the right side of the list that you might keep moving forward with God.

This is how you "abide in" Christ (John 15:4-7). Day by day and moment by moment, you turn from the mess in you to the goodness in him, praying, "Live through me, Lord Jesus."

Don't confuse your growth with getting something new from God you never had before. That's not how it works, because *everything* you need has already been lavished upon you in Christ.

Instead, the Exchanged Life plugs you in to the daily *experience* of those huge blessings. It's like having your name on the deed to a property and finally moving in. When I moved from my old house, to my present house, it took a while for my instincts to catch up. I'd leave my office, and turn the wrong way – toward my old house – for a few weeks. Old habits die hard. Consider the Exchanged Life your new habit of faith and rest.

Keep on trading in your bad stuff for his good stuff until it becomes your instinct.

Exchange your life.

By Faith

Galatians 2:20 unlocks the secret of how to activate this Exchanged Life: "the life I live... I live by faith in the Son of God..."

By faith.

Faith is the trembling hand laying hold of unshakable treasures. There is no magic. No superstitious chasing after an experience. No climbing a ladder of perfection or performing like a trained seal till your trainer throws you a fish.

There is simply a childlike faith in the work of Christ, not only for justification, but for sanctification too.

Does this mean passivity?

No, it means faith. Faith is the greatest struggle of your life. I would rather have you struggle to believe than struggle to obey, because if you win the struggle of faith, all other victories fall into place. "Faith is the victory," John said. "I live by faith," Paul declared. "Abide in me," Jesus taught – a sweet invitation to daily faith – and you will bear "much fruit" (1 John 5:4; Galatians 2:20; John 15:4,5).

Whatever sanctification is, it cannot be you grunting out holiness by your own efforts and strength. It is Christ's holiness, lived through you, by Christ's own power, or else it's just a pile of rotting fish. The more you strain, the less Christ sanctifies. But to the one who believes, "all things are possible" (Mark 9:23).

I hereby officially set you free from the wearying battle to be a good Christian. Instead, I send you forth to *believe* better, more deeply, and more widely in the matchless grace of God waiting for you in every trial, every adversity, and every circumstance of life. I warn you, the struggle of faith is tough. It requires maturity and a muscular endurance. But like all tough things in your life, Christ is your strength as you lean on him.

Keep on believing.

Because, if you do, you will wake up one day to find yourself on "God's great elevator carrying us up to the higher chambers of His palace, without arduous efforts, while others struggle up the winding stairs and faint by the way" (A.B. Simpson, opening quote of this chapter).

And you will say, "By Christ in me and his amazing grace, I am being sanctified."

Additional Scriptures

Ephesians 5:26, Romans 15:16, Acts 20:32, Exodus 31:13; Hebrews 2:11.

Prayer

Dear Lord,

You label yourself "The Lord Who Sanctifies." When I look in my heart and see the mess inside, I can only say Thank you, Lord, for not making me clean it up by myself. You roll up your sleeves and get to work. Lord, today I abide in Christ that the fruit of your Spirit might abide in me.

By faith, I trade my weakness for your strength, my poverty for your riches, and my sins for your righteousness. I rest in your power, not my own.

Hasten your sanctifying work in me, I pray.

Deliver me from addiction into dominion; make me free indeed.

Deliver me from dysfunctions into wholeness and health.

Deliver me from anxiety into a peace that passes understanding.

Deliver me from self-absorption into a love that never fails.

Lord Jesus Christ, shine through me today. Love through me today. Live through me today. Be Jesus in my speech, in my thoughts, in my instincts, in my feelings. Be my holiness, my courage, and my all in all.

I declare today that you are in me, and I am in you. I will rest in you as you work through me. I will strive by your power. I will rest my anxious heart even as I work my body, soul, and spirit to put bread on the table, and to care for those I love.

I declare this day a no-fear zone.

Today, I will walk in joyful holiness because I will walk in Christ.

Jesus, my job is faith; your job is being yourself through me. And I declare I can do all things through Christ who gives me strength.
In your Holy Name I pray,
Amen.

CHAPTER 23

I AM IN CHRIST

Meditation

There is no truth, therefore, more suited to impart confidence and strength, comfort and joy in the Lord than this one of union with Christ. It also promotes sanctification, not only because all sanctifying grace is derived from Christ as the crucified and exalted Redeemer, but also because the recognition of fellowship with Christ and of the high privilege it entails incites to gratitude, obedience, and devotion. ~John Murray[12]

Scripture

But of Him you are in Christ Jesus, who became for us wisdom from God – and righteousness and sanctification and redemption – that, as it is written, "He who glories, let him glory in the LORD." (1 Corinthians 1:30)

Bible Study

BOTH OF MY PARENTS SMOKED as I was growing up. I loved the smell. Every room in our house had ashtrays. It's weird for me to remember the days when ashtrays were a fashion statement. My dad smoked a pipe. He smoked little stubby cigars. And he always had a pack of Lucky's rolled up in his shirtsleeve.

Growing up, I loved that smell.

Today, I can't stand it. I'm not interested in judging anybody for smoking. Lord knows none of us can solve all our problems at once; we address our issues in baby steps.

My point is that when I lived in smoke, I liked the smell of smoke. But now that I've been out of smoke for a long, long time, I realize how bad the smell really is.

So it is with mistaken identity. When you live in it, you hardly realize how bad it smells. But once you get out of it, you look back and say, How did I ever live in that stuff?

The more tightly you identify with Christ, the more sensitized you are to anything that interferes with your identity.

You can gauge your growth in grace by your embrace of the labels God puts on you.

You can gauge your embrace of the Holy Spirit's presence by your confidence in who you are in Christ.

You can gauge the muscle on your faith by your everyday lifestyle that reflects the heart of Jesus in a way that draws others into his orbit.

We have been wrapping our minds around the epic truths of who we are in Christ. These are the deepest truths, the truest truths about us. This is reality – anything else is reality-lite.

I want to finish by putting it all together. I want to leave you with three steps to help you claim and experience what it means to be "in Christ."

Step One: Know

> Or do you not know that as many of us as were baptized into Christ Jesus were baptized into His death? (Romans 6:3)

Sometimes the old labels claim supremacy simply because you do not know the new ones. You haven't discovered your riches in Christ.

You do not know *who* you are.

You do not know *what* you have.

You do not know what Christ has done for you and become within you.

You do not know his matchless provision and his all-sufficient grace.

In 1982 a Japanese soldier emerged from the jungles of Guam. He had been hiding in the jungles for 37 years, since 1945. He did not know that World War 2 was over. So, for 37 years, he hid. He eked out his existence in isolation. The world passed him by, because he did not know.

I believe there is a crisis of biblical knowledge among God's people today. Every survey shows a gaping ignorance of even the most basic truths of the Christian faith. As church leaders, we are not doing a good job in our ministry of instruction.

Everywhere I go, Christians are up to speed with their duties and woefully ignorant of the stupefying riches bestowed on them to empower those duties.

The whole exhortation to a holy lifestyle is anchored in *knowledge.* You cannot live like Christ unless you think like Christ. And you cannot think like Christ unless you know your Bible, and specifically know your identity in Christ.

That is the foundation of all Christian living. That is the enabling power for you to make your everyday practice match your exalted position.

You can't love a God you don't know – how you label him is the most important thing about you.

You can't experience privileges and riches you don't know – how you label yourself is the second most important thing about you.

I wrote this book because I have great hope for Christ-followers who haven't yet discovered their riches in Christ. The possibilities blow my mind. Can you imagine the seismic culture-shift we'll see when millions of Christians finally unearth "the things that have been freely given to us by God" (1 Corinthians 2:12)?

If the people of God would quit limping beneath their dignity, if they would quit stooping beneath the weight of an endless succession of duties and obligations, if they would rise up to their true stature in Christ, the glory of Christ in them would dazzle the world with an utterly captivating glimpse of the matchless grace of God.

But it's not just enough to know. You also have to...

Step Two: Reckon

> Likewise you also, reckon yourselves to be dead indeed to sin, but alive to God in Christ Jesus our Lord. (Romans 6:11)

In frontier times in America, kids sent to one-room schoolhouses didn't do "math," they did "reckonings." This biblical word is a mathematical term. It means to do your calculations and reach a conclusion.

At the risk of stirring up scary memories of math-classes past, I'll remind you that doing math was a process. The answer only came after you crunched the numbers and reached a conclusion.

So it is with your *experience* of being in Christ. You are in Christ – that is reality. But you only *experience* life in Christ – feel it, sense it, enjoy it – as you have done the inner work of crunching your riches in Christ, absorbing them into your memory banks, rehabbing the mess inside, and installing God's own truth into your soul's operating system.

Reckoning drives your identity immeasurably deeper than "name it and claim it."

Knowing, step one, happens in your *mind* – at the surface level, in the academic realm of thinking, as you learn stuff by reading a book, or hearing a sermon.

Reckoning, step two, happens in your *heart* – at the deepest realm of instinct and feeling, as you declare God's truth, pray it, meditate on it, connect truth to truth, and believe it.

To reckon is to see yourself as God sees you. It is to make the calculation in which you say, I believe that what God has said about me is true, though a thousand voices scream my unworthiness.

The magic happens when you displace old, self-defeating mental scripts with new life-affirming biblical scripts. Doing this can feel like a mental wrestling match – a label-making cage-match. Bible study, Bible memorization, and prayer will make the difference.

On our family's last vacation, I lost my credit card halfway through the trip. Not even a determined search-operation could find it. My old mental labels immediately raised their grotesque little heads: *You're so stupid! How could you be so stupid?*

Five days later, I lost my drivers license after making it through airport security – a discovery I made only after flying across the blue Pacific. My old labels practically screamed: *See? Stupid! Stupid, stupid, stupid, stupid, stupid.*

I know I'm a pretty smart guy. On a deeper level, I know Jesus Christ became for me "wisdom from God" (1 Corinthians 1:30). God says I share Christ's wisdom. He says I "have the mind of Christ" (1 Corinthians 2:16). The "stupid" label doesn't apply.

Yet there it was, sticking to me like a gooey mess, with every search of our rented car, and with every repeated dismantling of my fat wallet.

Every failure tests who you reckon yourself to be.

It was time for me to reckon myself to be the wise, smart, capable person God says I am. So I did. I accepted

God's acceptance of me. It worked, because this was not just a superficial mantra for me; it was the activation of a long study in the same direction, of truths deeply embedded in my heart. My stress muscles unclenched, and peace reigned in my heart.

Know.

Reckon.

In the heat of the moment.

When the old labels scream their ownership of you. When voices from the past claw at your heart. Reckon yourself to be who God says you are in the heat of the moment, and you will see miracles happen. You will see the grace of God flood in.

You will see victory over temptations you never thought you'd beat.

You will see release from addictions you never thought you'd shed.

You will see deliverance from depressions and despair you never thought you'd conquer.

You will see courage rise up. Peace reign. Laughter in the teeth of the storm.

Hudson Taylor said, "All God's giants have been weak men who did great things for God because they reckoned on His being with them."[13]

That is the sweet power of reckoning.

Step Three: Yield

Therefore do not let sin reign in your mortal body, that you should obey it in its lusts. And do not present [yield] your members as instruments of unrighteousness to sin, but present [yield] yourselves to God as being alive from the dead, and your members as instruments of righteousness to God. (Romans 6:12,13)

Knowing happens in the mind.

Reckoning happens in the heart.

Yielding happens in the will.

In driving, yielding means letting the other driver go first. In your spirit, yielding means letting God's truth go first. It's a choice you make. It's faith on steroids.

When the dark voices of your past snarl and command you to obey, it is hard to push against that lifetime of deeply ingrained habits as they clamor for you to once again choose the path of least resistance. A giant habit inside longs to choose the low road; to pretend that nothing is different; to act as if you are the same old person you were before you met Christ.

But you're not.

Christ-in-you is reality, and everything else is reality-lite.

God doesn't exaggerate when he says sin is a deposed master. Even so, sin still clamors like a toothless lion to reign in your life.

You will yield to it or not. You will present yourself as an offering to it or not. You will either offer your services to sin or to God.

The choice is yours.

One way or another, you're going to yield to somebody. Every time you yield to God you strengthen your "identity muscles" and make yourself less vulnerable to the sleazy power of labels past.

But when you yield to sin, you have chosen the way of darkness and despair. You've served yourself up on a platter to forces that will gnaw at your joy like a rat on cheese.

You may have made that choice far too many times. You look back on your week or your month or many months, and shake your head. *I betrayed myself. I became my own worst enemy. My joy is wounded.*

Do you know why your joy is wounded?

Because your SELF is buried.

You must always go back to your true self, alive from the dead. You've been yanked up out of the graveyard of unsatisfying desires, depressing attitudes, and self-defeating habits.

You are alive in your true self to the God of all grace.

Yield in his direction.

The best Person who ever graced this worn out planet is alive and well within you. Every day, all day long, he will live through you, love through you, endure another day through you, rejoice through you, serve through you, and express his beautiful heart through you.

What incredible joy can be yours by yielding your mind, will, and emotions to the labels freely given by God!

Who Am I?

Hello, my name is Bill. I am a child of God, spiritual royalty, and a joint-heir with Jesus. I am destined to reign with him someday, but, until that day comes, I live by faith in the victory Christ has already won.

My sins are all forgiven.

My righteousness is utterly secure.

My salvation is everlasting.

My identity stands safe in his embrace.

You might know me as author, pastor, Chicago sports fan, friend, professor, or guy down the street. Heaven knows me as a shimmering receptacle of the glory of God.

The mightiest angels snap to attention when I walk through heaven's gates. They back away as I approach God's throne. They marvel that a flesh and blood mortal – frail, oftentimes failing, and all the time weak – would dare talk to God as I do. They clap their hands and wave their wings to cheer the mysterious decrees God makes in answer to my prayers.

People may look at me and scoff. They're not impressed. They see my imperfections. They call me stupid, too old, too young, too short, too fat, irrelevant. Dysfunctional. Not very tough. Not athletic. Not wealthy. They think I'm just another small-town guy caught in the same rat race as everyone else.

People have no clue.

Wherever I go, God goes with me. He shelters me with his omnipotence. A squad of angels watches over me.

The demons claw at me to bring me down, but God smacks them so hard, they can't scurry away fast enough.

Voices from my past seek to crush me. They flash my secret sins before my mind's eye. They throw my failures in my face. They spew forth reminders of the times I've let down my family, my church, and my God. But God's Spirit rises up to smash those voices into a slimy mess like flies on a swatter. *Your past is under the blood,* he reminds me. *And God has used you to bless countless lives in ways you can't understand this side of heaven.*

Frightening prospects of future disaster rise up to intimidate me – monsters of financial insecurity, ghosts of medical problems yet to come, fanged hordes of societal decay, and hellish beasts of wars on the horizon – yet Christ in me calms my anxious heart. *Let not your heart be troubled,* he says. *I've already been to the future. I've written the end of the story, and guess what... WE WIN!*

Who am I?

I am in Christ. I am forgiven. I am justified. I am reconciled. I am adopted. I am accepted. I am redeemed. I am blessed. I have an Advocate. I have access. I am complete in Him. I have power. I have dominion. I have a superpower. I am delivered from darkness. I am an heir of God. I am being sanctified.

God calls me beautiful, and beloved, and the apple of his eye.

Hello, my name is Bill, and I am in Christ.

Don't mess with me.

One Day

One day, the skies will be peeled back, your spirit and soul will be yanked from your decrepit body, earth will recede, and you will open your eyes in the realm where angels sing and golden streets glisten.

On that day, you will be what you were meant to be.

> Beloved, now we are children of God; and it has not yet been revealed what we shall be, but we know that when He is revealed, we shall be like Him, for we shall see Him as He is. (1 John 3:2)

"We shall be like him."

Remarkable. Unbelievable, if not for God's promise.

Like.

Him.

Just like Jesus in glory.

Just like Jesus in power.

Just like Jesus in beauty.

Just like Jesus in authority.

Just like Jesus in privilege.

Just like Jesus in wealth.

Just like Jesus in the warm embrace of his Father's love.

We shall be like him in experience.

Because we have been like him in status for all the years we've known him.

Every old label will be removed, shredded, and erased from heaven's memory banks. You will bask in the radiance of Christ's own glory. Even you – who wouldn't draw anybody's attention on earth – you will receive praise from God (1 Corinthians 4:5).

You will be just like Jesus in every way that matters.

On that day, your Union with Christ will be complete. Faith will merge with experience. Christ will be all in all. Such joy will overwhelm your heart, words can't express it, and your emotions can't contain it.

When Christ is put on display in his rightful glory, you will be put on display too. So great is your oneness with him, that even his glory will be yours.

> When Christ *who is* our life appears, then you also will appear with Him in glory. (Colossians 3:4)

This great Savior, whose hands and feet and brow still bear Calvary's scars, this all-wise teacher, this beloved friend, this humble man who healed and loved and served like no other... Jesus, your brother, your friend, your Savior, and your King... Every knee will bow before the celebrity of the Universe. Every tongue will praise him. What celestial fireworks! Praise will spontaneously erupt from our lips. Even the created order will add its applause. The roar of cosmic worship will rattle the gates of hell. And Jesus will have his rightful due.

And the greatest wonder of all, the mystery that no religion has ever conceived, the good news that makes our gospel the only gospel worthy of the name... is that when Jesus achieves that pinnacle of honor, he will share that self-same glory with you.

The veil that hides the real you will be torn away.

On that day, you will blaze forth in the true splendor of a child of God, an heir of salvation, and the crown royalty of heaven. The whole created order will stand on tiptoe to catch a glimpse of you, sparkling in your true glory (Romans 8:19).

You will be you, with all the color added.

You will be magnificent.

On that day, all creation will raise a shout in honor to you. But the greater praise will forever go to the One whose inexpressible love paid the unspeakable price of your incomparable salvation.

> His grace has planned it all,
> 'Tis mine but to believe,
> And recognize his work of love,
> And Christ receive.[14]

Additional Scriptures

Colossians 3:4, Romans 8:18, Psalm 31:19, 1 Corinthians 4:5.

Prayer

Gracious King,
I declare today that I am in Christ. One with him forever.
I am forgiven. I am justified. I am reconciled. I am adopted. I am accepted. I am redeemed. I am blessed. I have an Advocate. I have access. I am complete in Him. I have power. I have dominion. I have a superpower. I am delivered from darkness. I am an heir of God. I am being sanctified.

As He is before you, so am I.

No voice of defeat will own my thinking.

No failure of my past will drag me down.

No lies of the enemy will control my emotion.

No schemes of the devil will prosper against me.

No allurements of the world will seduce me from you.

My life is in Christ. So I find my hope in him, my abundance in him, my joy in him, and my satisfaction in him. No life will satisfy like a daily walk in him.

I declare myself to be what you say I am.

I declare myself to have what you say I have.

I declare myself to be going where you say I'm going.

My identity, my self-image, my personal worth, and my ultimate destiny are inextricably united to Jesus Christ.

I claim my triumphant spirit in Christ.

You have made me one with the most wonderful Person to ever walk this earth. In him you are well-pleased. In him, I am accepted without reservation.

Thank you for so great a salvation.

Thank you for so strong a hope.

Thank you for so wonderful a Savior.

By your grace, may I walk worthy of my high calling in Christ Jesus – one day at a time.

By his matchless grace, I pray,

And in the name of Jesus alone,

Amen.

Endnotes

[1] John Murray, *Redemption : Accomplished and Applied* (Grand Rapids: Eerdmans, 1955), p. 161.

[2] Bill Bright, The Four Spiritual Laws

[3] Malcolm Gladwell, *Blink: The Power of Thinking Without Thinking* (New York: Little, Brown, and Company, 2005), pp. 3-8.

[4] Gladwell, pp. 5,6.

[5] Gladwell, p. 7.

[6] Thayer's Greek Lexicon, public domain.

[7] http://www.foxnews.com/us/2014/02/25/california-couple-finds-10-million-in-rare-coins-while-out-walking-dog/ retrieved February 24, 2014.

[8] Gary Friesen, *Decision Making and the Will of God,* (Multnomah Press, 1982).

[9] John W. Peterson, "He Owns the Cattle," n.d.

[10] Dr. and Mrs. Howard Taylor, *Hudson Taylor's Spiritual Secret* (London: China Inland Mission, 1955), pp. 110–116.

[11] F.B. Meyer, *The Castaway and Other Addresses* (Chicago: The Bible Institute Colportage Association, 1897), pp. 95-96.

[12] Murray, p. 171.

[13] Dr. and Mrs. Howard Taylor, *Hudson Taylor and the China Inland Mission* (London: The China Inland Mission, reprinted 1921), p. 96.

[14] Norman J. Clayton, "My Hope is in the Lord." Public domain.

26580494R00120

Made in the USA
San Bernardino, CA
01 December 2015